Sing Me a Story

The Metropolitan Opera's® Book of Opera Stories for Children

Sing Me a Story

JANE ROSENBERG

Introduction by
Luciano Pavarotti

THAMES AND HUDSON

For Bob

Acknowledgments

For their invaluable assistance in the preparation of this book, I wish to thank JoAnn
Menashe Forman and Paul Gruber of the Metropolitan Opera Guild. My deepest
gratitude to my husband, Robert Porter, for his unfailing support. I am also indebted to
Marc Porter for allowing me access to his extensive opera library.

This book was prepared with the support and cooperation of the
Metropolitan Opera Guild

Copyright © 1989 by Jane Rosenberg
Introduction Copyright © 1989 by Luciano Pavarotti

First published in Great Britain in 1989 by
Thames and Hudson Ltd, London

Adaptation of *Amahl and the Night Visitors* by Gian-Carlo
Menotti is made by permission of Morrow Junior Books
(A Division of William Morrow and Company, Inc.)
Copyright © 1986 by William Morrow and Company, Inc.
Adaptation of and extracts from *Porgy and Bess* by George
Gershwin are made by permission of Warner/Chappell Music,
Inc. and Tams-Witmark Music Library, Inc. Copyright © 1935
by Gershwin Publishing Corp. Copyright renewed, assigned to
Chappell & Co., Inc.

Printed and bound in Singapore

Contents

Introduction

To sing for you would be the best way for me to introduce you **to**
which has been my career for almost thirty years. It was hea**ring**
when I was a boy that first brought me to opera—so in a way my **care**
my entire life. I grew up with it the way you grow up today with *Sta*
games. Opera was invented by Italians, and the music and stories **of**
of my home life. In fact, young people in Italy and all over Euro**pe**
with photographs of opera singers on them much the way people **no**
baseball players and other sports heroes.

Today it's different, and you are not likely to learn about ope**ra**
or teachers make a special effort. I have three daughters, and know **fr**
grow up that most young people care about what is the newest **thi**
song, the new television show, or the biggest new movie. In the la**st**
operas were written, they were truly the equivalent of the hit so**ng,**
and the effect on the people of that time was similar to the over**po**
have today from the mass media. Life did not move as fast then a**s it**
enjoy opera, you need to slow down just a bit. In that way you can **he**
the music and understand what is happening in the story.

And what marvelous stories they are! You'll meet kings and **q**
princesses, dwarfs, witches, wizards, and dragons—and for sure **y**
music good and evil, love and hate, and even war and peace. The**re**
and operas sad enough to make you cry. An opera can take place **in**
any time; it can send you on a trip to ancient Egypt, to the Paris of **a**
or to a place that never existed.

Most of the world's greatest composers wrote operas, and this **bo**
by Wolfgang Amadeus Mozart, Giuseppi Verdi, Richard Wagne**r,**

Contents

Introduction

To sing for you would be the best way for me to introduce you to the world of opera which has been my career for almost thirty years. It was hearing voices on records when I was a boy that first brought me to opera—so in a way my career has been almost my entire life. I grew up with it the way you grow up today with *Star Wars* movies and games. Opera was invented by Italians, and the music and stories of the opera were part of my home life. In fact, young people in Italy and all over Europe used to trade cards with photographs of opera singers on them much the way people now trade cards with baseball players and other sports heroes.

Today it's different, and you are not likely to learn about opera unless your parents or teachers make a special effort. I have three daughters, and know from watching them grow up that most young people care about what is the newest thing—the latest hit song, the new television show, or the biggest new movie. In the last century, when most operas were written, they were truly the equivalent of the hit song, movie or show—and the effect on the people of that time was similar to the overpowering feelings we have today from the mass media. Life did not move as fast then as it does today, and to enjoy opera, you need to slow down just a bit. In that way you can hear all the beauty in the music and understand what is happening in the story.

And what marvelous stories they are! You'll meet kings and queens, princes and princesses, dwarfs, witches, wizards, and dragons—and for sure you will hear in the music good and evil, love and hate, and even war and peace. There are comic operas, and operas sad enough to make you cry. An opera can take place in any country and at any time; it can send you on a trip to ancient Egypt, to the Paris of a hundred years ago, or to a place that never existed.

Most of the world's greatest composers wrote operas, and this book includes works by Wolfgang Amadeus Mozart, Giuseppi Verdi, Richard Wagner, Maurice Ravel, and

George Gershwin. These incredible men wrote music many years ago that can still excite and move us today. In most operas there is no spoken dialogue; all the words are sung, so the total effect is the music and words together which express what is happening along with the emotions that you can actually feel and hear in the theater.

Sometimes it is a problem that opera is sung in so many foreign languages—but believe me, even opera sung in English can sound like a different language. But if you learn the story of the opera, and take the time to listen to recordings or to watch videocassettes, you will be prepared in a better way, and your appreciation will grow as you recognize your favorite moments and feel the extraordinary power of grand opera. The more you know about opera, the more you will love it.

And then—you will want to go to a live performance. This is the most exciting: the sets and costumes, the sound of the orchestra, the experience of sharing with the rest of the audience. The next thing you know, you will be trying to go again!

I hope this book will lead you to the great enjoyment of opera—the sound of the human voice and the wonderful stories that are told. I hope that you will hear my voice along with all my colleagues who try to make opera a living art.

The next time I am on the stage—I will look for you in the audience.

Luciano Pavarotti

Act I

In ancient Egypt, where the gods control men's destinies, the young soldier Radames learns that Ethiopia may soon bring war on his country. He hopes that he may be chosen to lead the Egyptian army and dreams of returning victorious so that he can free his beloved Aida, an Ethiopian slave.

"Heavenly Aida, fair as a vision, you are the ruler of my whole life," he sings, and the rich melody of oboe and bassoon echoes his wish to help Aida return to her homeland.

As his song ends, Princess Amneris, daughter of the pharaoh, the king of Egypt, enters and begins to question Radames. She too is in love with the young warrior, but she suspects he loves someone else. Knowing he must conceal his feelings for Aida, the daughter of an enemy country, Radames speaks only of his wish to be named commander of the Egyptian army.

"Doesn't a more tender dream captivate your heart? A secret longing, perhaps?" she asks.

At that moment Aida enters the hall, and when Radames looks lovingly at her, Amneris's suspicions mount. Noticing that the girl has bowed her head to hide her tears, Amneris asks why.

"Alas! I hear the cries of war. What will befall my countrymen?"

"Does no deeper reason cause you sorrow?" asks the jealous princess.

The music races forward as Amneris, Radames, and Aida, standing apart, give voice to their inner thoughts. While Amneris secretly threatens her rival, Radames trembles at what their fate would be should the princess discover his love for the slave. And Aida, confessing the true reason for her tears, bemoans her hopeless love for the Egyptian warrior.

Trumpets signal the arrival of the pharaoh with his troops. The king announces that a messenger has come from the Ethiopian front.

"Egypt is invaded by the barbarous Ethiopians!" cries the messenger. "Our fields have been destroyed, and the plunderers are already marching on Thebes. A fearless warrior leads them: their king, Amonasro."

"Father!" gasps Aida, at the mention of his name. She realizes that now, more than ever, she must hide the secret of her royal birth.

At last, the pharaoh announces that the goddess Isis has chosen Radames to lead the army into battle, and the crowd cheers. As Aida watches apprehensively, the pharaoh commands Radames to don sacred arms in the Temple of Ptah. To a noble march, the king urges his troops on to victory—his song resounding with the grandeur of ancient Egypt.

"Return a conqueror!" Amneris sings, presenting the warrior with the battle standard.

Echoing her cry, the king and his subjects march off, leaving Aida alone in the great hall. In spite of herself, Aida has joined the cheering court. Now, she must confront her conflicting loyalties.

"Return a conqueror? How can I utter these words of betrayal?" she sings in self-reproach. "Behind his chariot I see my father in chains, my brother's blood spilled. O gods, destroy the army of our oppressors!"

But when she mentions her oppressors, she remembers Radames.

"How can I forget my love?" she sings tenderly. "Although I am a slave, this love has made me happy here."

In despair, Aida weeps and prays—first for her father, then for Radames. Raising her hands to the heavens, she begs the gods to pity her suffering, then drops to her knees.

*　　*　　*

The massive columns of the Temple of Ptah stand in long rows, receding dramatically from view. Statues of the gods tower over the altar where spirals of pale-blue smoke rise from burning incense. To the sound of harps, the priestesses pray to the god Ptah. Ramfis, the high priest, and his followers add their voices in praise, imploring the god to watch over the Egyptians.

Upon entering the temple, Radames is covered with a silver veil and presented with the sacred sword of Ptah. He prays to the god to bless and protect Egypt—a cry taken up by Ramfis and the priests.

"Almighty Ptah!" exults the entire chorus, raising their arms toward heaven.

Act II

In the perfumed air of Amneris's room in the royal palace at Thebes, the princess prepares to welcome the victorious Egyptian soldiers home from battle. To a

strumming harp, a chorus of slave girls sings a tribute to Radames, the conquering hero, as they cover Amneris in her golden ceremonial cloak.

When Aida enters, Amneris dismisses her servants. One look at the grieving slave girl and the princess's suspicions have returned. Determined to discover the truth, she pretends to be Aida's friend, urging her to live and be happy.

"Be happy? How can I, so far from my family and my defeated country?"

"Do you have other worries? Among the men who went to war against your country, do you fear for the safety of one?"

Tormented by Amneris's questioning, the slave girl regards her anxiously.

"A cruel destiny came only to a few men, our Radames among them," lies Amneris.

"Wretched fate!" Aida cries. "I'll weep forever."

Commanding Aida to look her in the eye, the princess admits: "I have deceived you . . . Radames lives!"

Aida falls to her knees and thanks the gods, her voice ringing out in relief and joy.

Alas, her involuntary confession is a fateful mistake—Amneris, relishing her triumph, sings out contemptuously.

"I love him too. The daughter of the pharaohs is your rival!"

Aida asks for Amneris's forgiveness, but the princess will not be appeased. As Aida begs for mercy, Amneris sings vengefully. In the distance a fanfare of trumpets and the victorious song of the army can be heard, heightening Amneris's triumph over the slave girl.

As the victors draw closer, Aida again begs for compassion. The tumultuous duet draws to a close when Amneris leaves for the ceremony and Aida, in despair, begs the gods to pity her fate.

*　　*　　*

Along a broad avenue at the entrance to Thebes, the Egyptians salute their pharaoh and his retinue: "Glory to Egypt and Isis!"

The army parades by to a triumphal march, while dancing slave girls display the captured Ethiopian treasures. Radames appears, drawn in a golden chariot, and the ecstatic crowd sings his praises. The king embraces the returning hero, and, dropping to his knees, Radames is crowned with the garland of victory by Amneris.

"Today your dearest wish shall be granted," declares the king.

Though wanting to ask for Aida's hand in marriage, Radames places his duty to her people first.

"Please have the prisoners brought before you," he asks the pharaoh.

Led in by guards, the prisoners file past. The last of the captives stands taller than the rest, and Aida recognizes her father, Amonasro. The Ethiopian king opens his arms to embrace his daughter, at the same time cautioning her not to reveal his rank.

"Who are you?" demands the pharaoh.

"I am Aida's father," replies Amonasro. "This uniform tells you that I defended my king and country."

In a majestic baritone, Amonasro eloquently describes the courage of his vanquished people. Then, humbling himself before the mighty Egyptian king, Amonasro begs him to be merciful. Joining her father's poignant song, Aida, too, pleads for the lives of her countrymen.

But their pleas are lost on Ramfis and the outraged priests who demand their deaths. The Egyptian populace, however, dismayed by the harsh sentence of the priests, cries out in favor of the vanquished. In a grand ensemble, everyone sings, expressing their most fervent hopes.

Radames reminds the king of his sacred promise and requests that the prisoners be set free. As a pledge of peace, Ramfis demands that Aida and her father be held hostage. The pharaoh agrees.

"Radames, your country's debt is unbounded. As your reward, you will marry Princess Amneris. One day you shall rule Egypt with her."

Radames dares not contradict the king, and Amneris smiles triumphantly at Aida. Amid a rejoicing chorus of delighted citizens, Aida's tragic voice can be heard.

"Alas, what hope is left me now? For him a glorious future, for me oblivion."

Taking her aside, Amonasro consoles his daughter. "Take heart, for the day of vengeance will soon dawn."

Act III

The temple of Isis stands on a summit overlooking the moonlit Nile. Disembarking from their barge, Amneris and Ramfis approach the temple. Chanting voices can be heard, praying to Isis and Osiris.

Ramfis counsels the princess to invoke the favor of the goddess Isis on the eve of her wedding. They enter the temple, followed by their guards and attendants.

As Aida's melancholy theme rises, the slave girl approaches. She looks around nervously, searching for Radames, who has asked her to meet him near the temple.

"I'm frightened. If Radames is coming to say farewell, the waters of the Nile will be my grave."

In a sorrowful song, Aida mourns the loss of her love and her country. With the approach of Amonasro, the music darkens, predicting the events to follow.

"I come with a solemn purpose, Aida," says her father. "If you wish it, you can conquer Amneris and the Egyptians."

Tempting his daughter with the promise of returning to her homeland, Amonasro assures her that there she can become the wife of Radames. He reminds her that Egypt has destroyed their homes and devastated their people.

"I still have an army and we are preparing to fight. One fact is needed to ensure our success: we must know the route our enemy will take."

Aida realizes that her father wants her to betray Radames. Horrified, she refuses.

The music resounds with fury as Amonasro cries out: "Even your dead mother curses you. You're not my daughter. You're the slave of the pharaohs."

"I'm still your daughter," she weeps.

"Remember, only through you can a conquered people live again."

Aida knows she must obey, but she is grief-stricken at the consequence.

"Courage, he's coming," whispers Amonasro, vanishing from sight.

Radames approaches, singing joyously. "At last I see you, sweetest Aida."

"Go away! The marriage rites of another love await you."

Radames wonders why Aida doubts his love until she asks how he can hope to avoid marrying Amneris.

"I'm off to war. Your people are arming for battle. When I return victorious, I'll reveal my heart to the king, and we'll be married."

Aida is convinced that they will be defenseless against Amneris's fury if Radames scorns her. She suggests another plan—to flee together to Ethiopia.

"My country will welcome us. With our love we'll forget the world."

At first, Radames is appalled at the thought of leaving his homeland. But he finally realizes that Aida is doomed if he refuses to marry Amneris, and he agrees to escape with her across the desert.

"We'll flee from this land of sorrow. Love will be our guide," they sing rapturously.

As they turn to leave, Aida pauses to ask a question. "By which route shall we avoid the army?"

"We need not worry. The road chosen will be deserted till morning."

"Which road is that?"

"The gorges of Napata."

"There I shall post my men!" exults Amonasro, emerging from the shadows.

Radames realizes to his horror that Aida's father is the leader of the Ethiopians.

"I am dishonored. I have betrayed Egypt."

Amonasro insists that fate willed this disclosure. As he urges Radames to escape with them, Amneris and Ramfis emerge from the temple and hear everything.

"Traitor!" screams Amneris, pointing at her betrothed.

Ramfis summons the guards while Radames begs Aida and her father to flee. Pursued by Egyptian soldiers, Amonasro drags Aida away, escaping into the night.

"Priest of Isis, I yield my sword," declares Radames, bowing before Ramfis.

Act IV

Amneris paces the palace hall near the cell where Radames awaits trial for treason. Although recognizing that Radames is not a traitor to his people, she nevertheless condemns him for wanting to leave with Aida.

"Death to them all!" she cries.

But in the next moment, love for Radames overwhelms her, and she resolves to save him. She asks the guards to bring the prisoner to her.

"Radames, your fate is about to be decided by the priests. Justify yourself and I will intercede."

"The judges won't accept excuses, nor do I feel guilty in the eyes of men or gods."

Plead as Amneris may, Radames rejects her offer of help.

"You wish me to live when you have slain Aida?"

"No, Aida lives! Though her father was killed in flight, she vanished without a trace."

Overjoyed, Radames prays for her safety, hoping she will never hear of his death. In a last effort to sway him, Amneris begs the warrior to renounce Aida and live. Radames, however, chooses death over life without his love.

"If I die for her, it will be a supreme joy," he declares, turning his back on the princess and returning to his cell.

The passionate music slows. Amneris blames herself for delivering Radames into the hands of his executioners, and watches in dread as the priests descend the stairs leading to the hall of justice.

Inside the hall, Ramfis reads the charges against the prisoner. Amneris listens intently.

"You revealed the secrets of your country to a foreigner. Defend yourself."

But Radames remains silent, and the court accuses him of treason.

"You deserted your camp the day before the battle. Defend yourself."

Again the priests are answered with silence.

"Radames, you have betrayed your country and your king. Defend yourself."

The priests await his defense but none is forthcoming, and they pronounce sentence.

"Beneath the altar of the god you've forsaken, you shall be entombed alive!"

*   *   *

Below the floor of the Temple of Ptah lies a dark crypt, soon to be Radames' tomb. He watches the last rays of light disappear as two priests lower a heavy stone to seal the vault.

A muffled sound startles Radames, and he discovers Aida kneeling in a corner.

"When the tomb was opened for you, I crept inside to die in your arms."

Though Radames mourns the fate she has chosen, he rejoices to hold her once more. Suddenly they hear the priestesses in the temple above. Their solemn chanting terrifies Aida, and Radames, unwilling to let her perish, tries in vain to move the stone that seals the vault. When the singing stops, peace returns to the dying lovers.

While the priestesses keep vigil, Amneris prostrates herself on the stones above the crypt. Below, Aida looks for the last time at Radames.

"Heaven opens for us!" they sing, and Aida dies peacefully in Radames' arms. Holding her tenderly, he follows her in death.

The curtain falls

GIAN CARLO MENOTTI

MOTHER

Amahl and the Night Visitors

KASPAR

BALTHAZAR

MELCHIOR

On the first Christmas Eve, along the road to Bethlehem, a crippled shepherd boy named Amahl sits outside his hut, playing a simple tune on his wooden pipe. Inside, his widowed mother weaves a rug and, after listening to Amahl's music for a time, calls him in to bed. But the boy finds it hard to tear himself away from the music and the star-filled sky. Losing patience with her disobedient child, the widow finally comes to fetch him.

"Mother, there has never been such a sky," he marvels. "All its lanterns are lit; all its torches are burning. There is a star that moves across the sky like a chariot on fire."

"You live in a dream. Here we are with nothing to eat, and all you do is worry your mother with fairy tales."

Dissonant chords on a piano accompany her anxious words. But still Amahl begs his mother to come outside and see the blazing star, and still she refuses to believe him, reminding him of the impossible things he claims to see every day.

The boy protests, and in his pure, sweet voice he sings, "Cross my heart and hope to die, I'm telling the truth."

Amahl's mother fears that hunger has gone to his head and is responsible for his strange tales.

"Our cupboards are empty. Unless we go begging, how shall we live through tomorrow?"

Amahl refuses to see a bleak future ahead and comforts the despairing woman. He paints a pretty picture of their life on the road—his mother dressed as a gypsy, himself as a clown. Spellbound by the child's story, the mother joins in his song. Then, tenderly kissing her son goodnight, she blows out the candle and they lie down on their beds of straw.

Moments later, Amahl, awake and restless, hears a trio of male voices, singing in the distance: "From far away we come, and far away we must go."

Limping to the window, he sees three men on donkeys approaching the hut. Soon, a loud knock at the door wakes the widow, who asks Amahl to see who it is. The boy opens the door and gasps at the royal visitor standing before him. He returns to his mother's bed and breathlessly sings: "Mother, come with me. I want to be sure that you see what I see—a king wearing a crown!"

His mother shakes her head sadly. "I'll have to spank you, if you don't tell the truth."

Amahl goes to the door again, and again he returns to his mother's bedside.

"Mother, come with me. I want to be sure that you see what I see—there are two kings!"

Still refusing to believe Amahl's tale, she watches as her son opens the door a third time. Even Amahl is amazed by what he sees.

"Mother, you won't believe me. There are three kings outside!"

Amahl's mother finally rises from her bed to see. There, in majestic splendor, stand three richly garbed kings. They sing "Good evening" in harmony and politely ask to rest by her fire.

"A cold fireplace and a bed of straw are all I can offer you, but you are welcome to them," she humbly replies.

To a spirited march, they enter the hut, followed by their page. The kings seat themselves on three stools, while the page unrolls an oriental carpet and spreads their treasures before them.

The widow steps outside to borrow firewood from the neighbors, warning Amahl not to disturb their guests. But the moment she closes the door, Amahl scurries to the side of the Nubian king, Balthazar, and peers curiously into his face.

"Are you a real king?"

"Yes," answers Balthazar, smiling kindly.

"Do you have royal blood?"

"Yes, and it's just like yours."

"What's the good of having it then?"

Amused by the boy's sincerity, King Balthazar asks him what he does. Amahl explains that once he was a shepherd with a flock of sheep and a black goat that gave warm, sweet milk.

"But my mother sold the sheep and the goat died of old age."

The three kings feel a twinge of pity. But when, without complaining, Amahl explains that he will soon go begging, their pity turns to admiration for the boy's courage.

Amahl's attention is diverted by King Kaspar, who is playing with a parrot in a silver cage. When the boy wonders what the wooden box next to Kaspar contains, the king describes its contents.

"The first drawer has magic stones to guard against evil. The second holds precious beads, and in the third I keep licorice. Have some!"

Amahl accepts the delicious sweet, but when his mother returns to the hut, he hides it guiltily. The widow suspects that he has been making a nuisance of himself.

"Off you go! Ask the other shepherds to bring whatever food they can for our guests."

Amahl hobbles out on his wooden crutch. In his absence, his mother admires a large chest sitting on the carpet. When King Melchior opens the lid, the poor woman stares in awe at the piles of gold and precious gems.

"These are gifts for the Child," explains Melchior.

"The child?" she whispers. "What child?"

To a magical melody, King Melchior sings, "Have you seen a Child the color of wheat, the color of dawn? His eyes are mild, his hands are those of a king, as king he was born."

The widow answers him in her beautiful soprano: "Yes, I know a child the color of wheat, the color of dawn. 'Tis my child."

The kings had hoped she would be able to guide them to the Child of their vision. She senses their disappointment now, but none could be sadder than the helpless mother of a hungry, crippled boy.

Gazing out of the window, she watches the shepherds and their families follow Amahl to the hut. They carry baskets laden with nuts and fruit and shyly offer their simple gifts to the kings.

The widow coaxes the young people to dance for her guests, and they perform a lively tarantella. At the end of the dance, King Balthazar, rising from his seat, thanks the shepherds and bids them goodnight. The kings, he explains, need sleep for the long journey ahead. Singing goodbye, the shepherds take their leave.

In the silence that follows, Amahl whispers in King Kaspar's ear: "Sir, among your magic stones, is there one that could cure a crippled boy?"

"Eh?" responds the half-deaf old king.

"Never mind," sighs the boy, and limps wearily to his bed.

His mother, who has heard Amahl's request, snuffs the candle and stares sadly into the darkness. The three kings fall fast asleep.

As the night passes, the woman stares fixedly at the treasure chest.

"All that gold," she sings over and over. "Do they know that a starving child could be fed with a little of their gold?"

Feeling it unjust to bestow so much wealth on an unknown child while her own goes hungry, she creeps silently toward the treasure chest.

"For my child," she repeats again and again. Finally, her hand clasps a bag of gold.

The page immediately awakens. Seizing the woman, he cries out, "Thief!" and wakes the others.

Amahl flings himself at the page, and, to furious chords, he sings, "Don't you dare hurt my mother!"

Pounding the page's back, the desperate child begs Kaspar to make the servant release his mother. The old king motions to the page, and the frantic music slows to a soothing melody. Amahl drops to the floor beside his mother, and she rocks him in her arms.

Full of compassion, King Melchior insists they keep the gold.

"The Child we seek doesn't really need our gold. He will build his kingdom on love alone." And turning to leave, he bids his companions to follow.

"No! Wait . . . take back your gold," the widow begs, rising to her feet. "I've waited all my life for such a king. If I weren't so poor, I would send a gift of my own."

Amahl, drying his tears, wishes to send a gift as well. The music stops, anticipating the child's great sacrifice.

"Mother, let's send him my crutch. He may need it."

Amahl lifts the crutch from under his arm, but instead of falling he miraculously steps forward. Unable to believe what has happened, he tries another step. His mother rushes to his side and embraces him.

"This is a sign from God," the kings sing with hushed reverence.

"Look, Mother, I can jump, I can run!"

While the kings laugh merrily, Amahl dances about the room. His mother cautions him to be careful, but the kings assure her that he is cured.

Amahl's thoughts turn again to the Child, and he begs his mother to allow him to present his crutch in person. When the kings promise to take good care of the boy and bring him home safely, Amahl's mother consents.

As Amahl leaves with the kings and their page, the shepherds gather outside the hut. The widow stands at the door and blows kisses to her son, while he plays his wooden pipe and walks out of sight on his two strong legs.

The curtain falls

Amahl and the Night Visitors

THE
BARBER OF SEVILLE
ROSSINI

Rosina   Figaro   Almaviva   Berta   Basilio   Bartolo

Act I

Count Almaviva has fallen in love with the breathtakingly beautiful Rosina during a chance meeting in Madrid and has followed her home to Seville. As dawn breaks, he lingers beneath her window, hoping to catch a glimpse of his love.

His servant, Fiorello, has assembled a band of musicians, and they accompany the count as he serenades Rosina: "Awake, my love. Soothe the pain of Cupid's dart."

When Rosina fails to appear on her balcony, Almaviva fears his suit is hopeless. At last, he dismisses the musicians and sends Fiorello away. He continues his vigil alone, but his thoughts are soon interrupted by a voice singing merrily in the distance. Almaviva hides in the shadows under Rosina's balcony.

Figaro, the barber of Seville, saunters down the cobblestone street with a guitar slung over his shoulder. In a robust baritone the cheerful barber sings of the good fortune life has bestowed upon him.

"I am respectable, highly acceptable; in any circle, I feel at home. I am reliable, clever, and pliable; I am the king of lather and foam."

Thumbing through his diary, Figaro boasts of how his skills are always in demand, be it for a shave, to powder a wig, to apply a leech, or to deliver a message involving delicate matters of the heart.

"Night and day, I'm needed everywhere, wanted by everyone. Figaro, Figaro, Figaro," he cries, mimicking the shouts of his clients.

Count Almaviva, realizing that this man's services could be of use, approaches the barber. Figaro immediately recognizes the nobleman, despite the simple cloak he wears, and bows graciously.

"Excellency," he booms.

"Hush! No one must know who I am. But I depend on you to assist me in my plans."

Almaviva explains that he has followed a girl home from Madrid, the daughter of Dr. Bartolo.

"What luck!" Figaro cries. "I attend Dr. Bartolo. I am his barber, valet, surgeon, chemist, masseur, and resident busybody. And what's more, your beloved is not his daughter—she is merely his ward."

Hearing footsteps, the two take cover in the shadows. The lovely Rosina appears on the balcony, looking for her admirer, and Almaviva leaps out of hiding to greet her.

Rosina has written an encouraging letter and is about to hand it to the count when Dr. Bartolo, an aging, avaricious tyrant, follows her onto the balcony. Figaro grabs Almaviva by his collar, pulling him back into the shadows.

"What is that paper you're holding?" the doctor demands of Rosina.

"Oh, it's nothing, just an aria from the latest opera—*The Useless Precaution*."

Waving the letter nervously, Rosina drops it over the side of the balcony. Dr. Bartolo rushes into the house and heads for the door, but Rosina quickly motions to her suitor to pick up the note. Almaviva and Figaro retrieve the letter, hiding just in time. The old doctor stalks out of the house and scours the pavement.

"Where is it, Rosina?"

"The wind must have blown it away."

"Go inside," he orders angrily. "Tomorrow, I'll brick up that balcony."

When the doctor returns to the house, Figaro and the count creep out of the shadows. Almaviva reads Rosina's letter aloud.

"'As soon as my guardian leaves, let me know your name, rank, and intentions. Though the tyrant forbids me to appear on the balcony alone, I'll do my best to break the chains that bind me. Your unhappy Rosina.'"

They barely finish the letter when Dr. Bartolo appears at the door, and, once again, the conspirators retreat into the shadows. Bartolo instructs his servant Ambrogio to keep Rosina under lock and key and to admit no one but Don Basilio, the music master.

"I'll marry Rosina myself tomorrow, before anyone else can get his hands on her inheritance," he states emphatically and marches off.

Figaro now urges the count to serenade Rosina, making his intentions clear. While the barber strums his guitar, Almaviva sings a lyrical love song. Because he wants Rosina to love him for himself, and not for his title and wealth, he decides to use an assumed name.

"I am Lindoro who adores you, who wants you for his wife. Though I cannot give you riches, my heart is yours forever."

Rosina's sweet voice rings out in response: "My heart is yours and. . . ."

Before she can utter more, she is pulled away from the balcony window. Almaviva begs Figaro to find a way to sneak him into the house. When the barber hesitates, the count promises to reward him in gold. Figaro springs into action, singing merrily to a chorus of strings.

"The thought of precious metal and my brain begins to work. I know—we'll disguise you as a soldier and you'll be billeted in Bartolo's house by military order!"

Pleased as Punch with his scheme, Figaro unleashes a torrent of self-congratulation.

Act I

THE
BARBER OF SEVILLE

"I'm a genius! What invention! I'm a veritable magician."

The barber promises to find Almaviva a suitable uniform, and the happy count sings a final duet with his accomplice before they part—Almaviva glorying in love, Figaro reveling in money.

*   *   *

Rosina dips a quill into an inkwell and writes her suitor a second note. Singing of her love for Lindoro, she vows to use her wit and wiles against the objections of her guardian.

"I am sweet, obedient, loving, and compliant. But if I'm thwarted, I'm a viper."

She wonders aloud who can be trusted to deliver her letter to Lindoro. Just as she mentions the barber's name as a possible go-between, he quietly enters the room. With evident satisfaction, Figaro listens to Rosina's comments before making his presence known.

Rosina bids the barber good morning, but as they are about to share confidences, Dr. Bartolo walks in. Figaro scurries away, promising to speak with her later.

"Have you seen Figaro?" asks Bartolo.

"If it will upset you—the answer is yes!" Rosina retorts, leaving the room in a huff.

"I don't trust that barber. I'm sure he's poisoning her mind against me."

On the other hand, Don Basilio, the music master, is a trusted companion. He enters the drawing room now with news of great importance: the famous Count Almaviva is in town and has been secretly courting Rosina. When Dr. Bartolo bitterly complains, Basilio puts forth a plan of his own. He suggests slander as a means to discredit Almaviva, thereby destroying his chances with Rosina.

As Figaro sneaks back into the drawing room and hides behind a potted plant, Don Basilio describes the subtle art of slander.

"Slander is like a little breeze—gentle and imperceptible."

He creeps stealthily around the room as he describes how slander grows from murmur to whisper to din to thunder as gossip roars with the fury of a firing cannon. Though Dr. Bartolo appreciates the subtlety of the plan, he prefers to draw up the marriage contract immediately—the quickest means to reach his ends. Basilio, unabashed at the rejection of his own scheme, is happy and willing to assist.

"If the money is right, I'll do anything," he says, following the doctor from the room.

Figaro smiles slyly at what he has overheard. Rosina returns, and the barber informs her that Bartolo is making plans to marry her the very next day.

"He'll live to regret it!" she storms.

Figaro urges her to hurry and write Lindoro a brief note as a sign that she wishes to see him again.

"It's already done," replies Rosina.

The barber admires her cunning—equal only to his own. Singing together, Rosina celebrates her good fortune in love, while Figaro puzzles over the ways of women—wily and sly beneath their mild exteriors. Figaro then leaves to deliver her message, and Rosina lolls happily on the couch.

Dr. Bartolo enters, taking Rosina by surprise. Hastily, she picks up her embroidery and pretends to be busy.

The old man accuses her of writing a love letter and questions every detail of her activities, but the quick-witted girl has a dozen excuses. Unable to get an honest answer from her, Bartolo bursts into an exasperated aria, his powerful voice booming with suppressed rage. When Rosina refuses to confess, her guardian threatens to lock her in her room.

But he is no match for the stubborn Rosina. His threats have no effect on her, and he leaves in a huff, followed by his ward, who skips blithely out of the room.

Sneezing and wheezing, Berta, the old housemaid, enters and sets down a basket of laundry beside the couch. Before she has time to pick up her broom, a loud knock on the door calls her away. Military music introduces Almaviva, disguised as a drunken soldier.

The impostor, in full-dress uniform, stumbles into the drawing room and shouts for the master of the house. When Berta, in alarm, ushers Dr. Bartolo into the room, Almaviva is reclining on the desk, gulping brandy from a silver flask.

"Dr. Barbarous, I presume," mocks the soldier, waving his orders under the old man's nose. "I am to be quartered in your house."

As an outraged Bartolo reads the orders, Rosina enters. The count reveals himself to her as Lindoro, and Rosina begs him to be careful. Almaviva, edging closer to his sweetheart, attempts to pass a note to her, but he inadvertently drops it. When he manages to pick it up and give it to Rosina, Bartolo catches them in the act and insists on seeing the paper.

"You are welcome to see the paper, sir," Rosina offers, substituting a laundry list from Berta's basket for the love note. "But your suspicions are unbearable!"

Almaviva, springing to her defense, threatens to cut the doctor's throat. Berta shows

Basilio into the drawing room, and soon everyone is shouting. Figaro, hearing the commotion from the street, enters and tries to restore peace. But the name-calling and threats continue until suddenly a loud knock at the door startles them all into silence.

"Open in the name of the law!"

"Now we are done for!" everyone cries.

The militia enter with their weapons pointed, demanding to know the reason for the ruckus. First Bartolo, then Figaro, then everyone in turn addresses the commanding officer until the entire party is chattering and singing at once. The officer finally determines that the drunken soldier is responsible and orders his men to arrest the culprit.

"Arrest me? Impossible!" says Almaviva, taking the officer aside and identifying himself.

When the officer realizes he has been addressing a nobleman, he drops to his knees in amazement and orders his men to stand at attention. Everyone in the house, except for Figaro, is spellbound by this turn of events.

Then, as bells chime and flutes pipe, one and all sing: "My poor head is madly reeling, like a mighty millstone wheeling, till my throbbing brain is numb."

Act II

That evening, Dr. Bartolo sits alone in the music room, sipping a glass of wine. A knock on the door interrupts his thoughts. Almaviva, disguised in spectacles, a gray hat, and a black coat, enters the room.

"Heaven bless you," he warbles in an oily, ingratiating voice. "I am Don Alonso, professor of music and pupil of Don Basilio. Since the master is indisposed, he sent me in his place."

Dr. Bartolo is very suspicious, and Almaviva knows he must do something to prove his sincerity or else risk being dismissed as an impostor. He reluctantly produces one of Rosina's notes, which he claims to have stolen from the count.

Snatching the letter from Almaviva's hand, Bartolo runs off to call his ward, and returns with her a few moments later. When the old man looks the other way, the count

Act II

THE
BARBER OF SEVILLE

gallantly tips his hat and peers over his spectacles, revealing his identity to Rosina.

"Come sit beside me at the piano and I'll give you your lesson."

Rosina happily obliges, informing her guardian that she intends to sing an aria from *The Useless Precaution*.

"The heart aflame with love does not fear the tyrant," she sings pointedly. "Love will always triumph."

Dr. Bartolo sits down in a comfortable chair and is soon dozing. Rosina, taking advantage of his inattention, begs the man she knows as Lindoro to rescue her from Bartolo's clutches.

"Have no fear," he assures her tenderly. "We'll find a way."

When the old man stirs, Rosina jumps up and resumes her song, her lovely voice rippling up and down the scale. Both men applaud, but Bartolo offers only qualified praise.

"Beautiful, but boring. In my day, music was different."

He sings a minuet from his youth and performs a few delicate steps of the dance. Figaro, entering silently with his shaving bowl, observes the doctor's pretty dance and imitates his steps with exaggerated grace and delicacy.

"What are you doing here?" demands Bartolo, insulted by the barber's mimicry.

"I've come to give you a shave," answers Figaro, removing his jacket and rolling up his sleeves.

Bartolo reluctantly agrees, and he hands Figaro his key ring, instructing him to find some towels in the linen closet. Soon after Figaro leaves the room, the sound of breaking china is heard. Dr. Bartolo runs off to the linen closet, leaving just enough time for Almaviva to propose marriage and Rosina to accept.

Figaro and the doctor return; and while Figaro, in his defense, complains that the closet was too dark to see the china, he secretly passes Almaviva the balcony key that he has slipped off the ring.

Dr. Bartolo sits down to be shaved when, to the consternation of all, Don Basilio, in perfect health, enters the room.

"Do you feel better?" asks Bartolo.

"In what way?" wonders Basilio.

Almaviva looks sympathetically at Basilio and asks him why he is up and about with a fever.

The confused music master scratches his chin. "Something is fishy here."

Figaro measures Basilio's pulse. "You're trembling. And your pulse is racing. It's a case of scarlet fever!"

"You need a good tonic," advises Almaviva, handing him a purse of coins.

The diagnosis is unanimous, and everyone urges Basilio to go home to bed. Finally taking the hint, and the money, he leaves, and Almaviva and Rosina sit down again at the piano.

Figaro ties an apron around Dr. Bartolo's neck, slyly making a few loops through the back of the chair, and begins to lather his client's face.

Almaviva promises Rosina to come for her at midnight, and tries to explain that he had no choice but to give her letter to Bartolo.

"I had to protect my disguise," he begins, but they are interrupted. Hearing the word "disguise," Bartolo has suddenly put two and two together.

"Rogues! Vagabonds!" he shrieks, attempting to free himself from the chair.

Figaro, Rosina, and Almaviva playfully sing, "You're delirious!" as he tries to walk with the chair strapped to his back. Then, laughing and rejoicing, they run from the room, leaving a furious Bartolo tied to his seat.

The old tyrant yells for Berta, who rushes in with Ambrogio to untie her master. Bartolo orders Ambrogio to fetch Basilio, and, when the music master arrives, Bartolo discovers he knows nothing of Alonso.

"Then the count must have sent him," deduces Bartolo.

"He must *be* the count!" responds Basilio. "The money he gave me proved it. Only the rich Almaviva would give away so much so casually."

"That's it—I'm calling the notary. I'll marry Rosina tonight."

After sending Basilio to fetch the notary, Bartolo calls Rosina. She enters to find her guardian impatiently tapping his foot and holding a piece of paper—her letter.

"Your love is merely toying with you," he declares triumphantly. "Lindoro and Figaro are scheming to procure you for their master, Count Almaviva."

Angered and disillusioned by what she feels is Lindoro's betrayal, Rosina offers to marry her guardian at once. Bartolo, scarcely believing his ears, rushes to her side and kisses her hand in assent.

Rosina then discloses Lindoro's scheme to enter the house at midnight by way of the balcony. Planning to take revenge on his rival, the doctor retires to his study.

"What a cruel fate!" Rosina sobs, as she disconsolately follows her guardian from the room.

*   *   *

Outside the house, a storm howls. Streaks of lightning, visible through the balcony shutters, light up the midnight sky as the music thunders and rolls.

Almaviva and Figaro have scaled a ladder to the balcony. Turning the key, the count enters the drawing room, followed by the barber.

"Where's my dear Rosina?"

"Stand back!" she cries, entering the room. "You pretend to love me, only so that you might sacrifice me to your wicked friend, Almaviva!"

Delighted to know that Rosina has no interest in the wealthy count but loves only Lindoro, Almaviva reveals his true identity. Rosina realizes that love was his only motive for concealing his position, and unhesitatingly forgives the count with all her heart.

With his usual lack of modesty, Figaro sings, "Now they die of joy, and it is all thanks to me!"

The count promises Rosina to make her his wife. So happy and distracted are they, that Figaro cannot induce them to flee.

"*Andiamo!*" the barber cries for the tenth time, and Almaviva is finally convinced of the imminent danger.

They consider escaping down the ladder, but their discussion costs them precious time, and the ladder disappears before their very eyes.

With the notary in tow, Don Basilio marches into the room. Figaro takes charge and, pretending to be Dr. Bartolo, introduces Rosina as his niece and Almaviva as her betrothed. To prevent Basilio from revealing the deception, the count bribes him with a diamond ring.

In haste, Rosina and Almaviva sign the marriage contract, which is witnessed by Figaro and sealed by the notary.

Almaviva kisses his bride, while Figaro hugs Basilio.

In the midst of the celebration, Dr. Bartolo, followed by an officer and his squadron, marches into the room.

"Arrest the thieves!" yells the doctor.

"Your name!" bellows the officer, turning to Almaviva.

When the count reveals his real identity, the entire room is speechless—all except for Bartolo, who continues to protest. But the count, with the authority of his rank, proclaims that Bartolo's tyranny is at an end and that his marriage to the mistreated Rosina is binding.

In despair, the doctor declares himself a fool for removing the ladder and thus hastening their marriage.

"A useless precaution," Figaro chuckles.

Almaviva waives his claim to Rosina's dowry, leaving it, instead, to the doctor, which makes Bartolo feel much better.

"I get the money. You get the girl and my blessings."

"That's the spirit!" Figaro sings joyfully. "Let us cherish, one and all, our memories of this night."

And everyone joins Figaro in a rollicking chorus, hailing the happy couple and their future.

The curtain falls

Mimi   Rodolfo   Schaunard   Musetta

Colline   Marcello

Act I

In a dusty garret overlooking the rooftops of Paris, the painter Marcello works on his latest canvas. His roommate Rodolfo, a poor poet, stares out of the window at the smoking chimneys of the Latin Quarter.

"Look how the smoke floats up from stoves all over Paris, yet our stove lies idle."

"My fingers are frozen, and there's no money for firewood," answers the painter, "but this chair will be our salvation."

Marcello is about to break the chair into kindling when Rodolfo offers to burn his play instead. He fetches a heavy manuscript and hands Marcello the first act. Together, they throw the pages into the stove and gaily set fire to them.

A third roommate, Colline, enters the garret in a foul temper.

"Christmas Eve, a night when a man needs money, and not a single pawnshop is open."

"Hush! My drama is on," commands Rodolfo, pointing to the fire. He shreds the rest of his manuscript and feeds the flames, but the fire soon dies out.

"A short-lived drama," observes Colline.

"Down with the author!" sing his two critics as they chase the poet about the room.

The door flies open and two delivery boys enter, carrying firewood, food, wine, and cigars. They are followed by Schaunard, the final member of this quartet, who smiles proudly at his friends.

"I was hired by a wealthy English lord to give him music lessons, but when I arrived I was told to play my horn for a parrot and not to stop until the troublesome bird had died. And so I played, exhausted, for three whole days till a sweet servant girl helped me feed it parsley laced with arsenic."

Meanwhile, barely listening to his tale, Schaunard's starving friends begin feasting. When the musician finally notices they are devouring the ham and the Christmas pudding, he intercepts a platter of food.

"Why should we stay indoors when the cafés of the Latin Quarter are offering mouth-watering delicacies? We may drink at home," he sings merrily, filling their glasses with wine, "but we're dining out."

A knock at the door brings the festive music to a sudden halt.

"It's Benoît," a whining voice calls.

"Oh no! The landlord!" cries Marcello.

"Give me one word," pleads the old man.

"All right, but just one," they agree, opening the door.

"Rent!" demands Benoît, waving a bill before them.

Suddenly courteous, Marcello offers the landlord a seat and a glass of wine. No sooner does Benoît empty his glass than Schaunard refills it, offering toast after toast. Declaring he looks like a young man, the Bohemians appeal to his vanity, calling him a Don Juan. Benoît is flattered and admits to having a weakness for pretty women.

Pretending to be outraged, the young men cry, "What? This man leads a scandalous life! Drive the wretched sinner out!" Caught off guard, the drunken Benoît is pushed out of the door with not so much as a sou of the rent money.

"And now," says Schaunard, hastily dividing his earnings among his friends, "it's time to go to the Café Momus."

Schaunard, Colline, and Marcello put on their threadbare coats, but Rodolfo sits down at the table with pen and paper.

"I'll be along in five minutes. I must finish writing my article."

Alone, Rodolfo tries to work, but he can only stare at the blank page. A knock on the door offers a welcome distraction.

"Forgive me. Would you light my candle? I can't find my way," says the young woman standing on the threshold. She presses a handkerchief to her mouth and coughs hoarsely.

"You're ill. Please come in."

As the stranger enters the room, she nearly faints, dropping her candle and a key. Rodolfo helps her to a chair, but she is too weak to sit upright and collapses at the table. Alarmed, Rodolfo splashes a few drops of water on her face, and she revives.

"Warm yourself by the fire," he insists, charmed by her tragic beauty.

He offers her a glass of wine, which she gratefully accepts. Then, retrieving the candle from the floor, Rodolfo lights the wick.

The young woman rises to leave and, when they reach the door, pauses to search the pockets of her skirt.

"I can't find my key," she tells him as the music weaves a spell of enchantment around the couple.

Rodolfo, concealing his delight, searches the room with her. He discovers the missing key but hides it in his pocket. They continue looking and, by chance, their fingers touch. The poet draws her hand into his and presses it close to his heart.

"How cold your little hand is. Let me warm it in mine. As for your key, we'll wait till

the moon rises and the light is stronger. Then we'll find it."

Rodolfo now introduces himself and, his voice rising in song, tells about his life, his work, his hopes, and his dreams.

"Since you now know me, won't you tell me who you are?"

"They call me Mimi. I earn my living sewing and embroidering." But when she sings of the lilies and roses she creates, she reveals herself to be more than a seamstress: she, too, is a poet.

Rodolfo hears his friends calling from the street, and he leans out of the window to explain his delay. When they learn the poet has company, they agree to go ahead and reserve a table at the café.

Watching the moonlight play upon Mimi's hair, Rodolfo sings of his happiness at finding someone to love. Mimi, too, sings of a heart awakened by love. Then, arm in arm, they leave to join Rodolfo's friends.

Act II

In the square outside the Café Momus, last-minute shoppers crowd the sidewalks while vendors sell flowers, books, and bric-à-brac. Mimi and Rodolfo emerge from a hat shop, where Rodolfo has bought her a pink bonnet as a token of his love. As they make their way through the crowd, two handsome students tip their hats to Mimi, and one kisses her hand. This small gesture of admiration sparks Rodolfo's jealousy.

"You're flirting, Mimi. A man in love is always suspicious."

"Are you in love, then?"

"Forever!"

At last, the Bohemians join one another at an outdoor table overlooking the square. Rodolfo formally introduces Mimi to his friends, declaring that he may be a poet but that she is poetry itself: "Here in my mind blossom the verses, and from her fingers blossom the flowers. Together, love blossoms from our hearts."

After poking fun at Rodolfo's flowery oration, Colline, Marcello, and Schaunard offer a friendly welcome to Mimi. Then, amidst the delightful Christmas-Eve chaos in the square, they merrily order omelets, capons, lobsters, and wine. Schaunard and Colline raise their glasses and propose a toast: "Down with despair, life is fair!"

Everyone drinks but Marcello, who watches as his former sweetheart, the singer Musetta, alights from a carriage. Following her, and laden with parcels, is her elderly admirer, Alcindoro. The singer, confident of her power over the old man, orders him about like a servant, and, against Alcindoro's wishes, she claims a table opposite the Bohemians. Leaning back flirtatiously in her chair, she pretends to ignore Marcello.

"What a lovely dress she's wearing," exclaims Mimi. "Who is she?"

"Her first name is Musetta. Her last name: Temptation!" Marcello replies bitterly, trying his best to ignore her.

Musetta has decided that Alcindoro is really an old bore, and she longs to be reunited with Marcello. To attract his attention, she lifts her dinner plate in the air.

"Waiter!" she shouts. "The plates are dirty."

Marcello continues to ignore her. This is more than Musetta can bear, and she smashes one dish after another on the ground.

"Quiet! Hold your temper. Not so loud," whimpers Alcindoro.

"I'll do as I please," she tells him, peeling off her long satin gloves and strolling toward a group of soldiers.

While a waltz plays, Musetta enchants the soldiers by singing a lyrical tribute to her own beauty and charms: "When I walk by, men turn to admire and praise me. They gaze at me wherever I go."

Alcindoro is embarrassed by her behavior, but Musetta continues her song, knowing her triumph over Marcello is at hand. In order to get rid of the old man, she pretends that her shoe is pinching and demands that he buy her a new pair. As Alcindoro hurries away, Musetta confronts Marcello.

"I love you still," he admits.

"My Marcello!" she cries, throwing her arms around him.

At that moment, the waiter brings the bill to the artists' table. One after the other, the four men check their pockets. Much to their surprise, they've spent every bit of Schaunard's earnings.

Distant sounds of piccolos, trumpets, and drums are heard as Musetta snatches the bill, adds it to Alcindoro's tab, and explains to the waiter that her companion will pay everything when he returns.

"I'll leave this as a farewell gift," she winks.

As a marching band draws near, the crowd lines up to make way for the parade. Knowing this is their chance to escape before Alcindoro returns with Musetta's shoes, Marcello and Colline lift the singer onto their shoulders. The merry party disappears into a crowd of Parisians who hail, "Viva Musetta, queen of our hearts!"

Act III

On the outskirts of Paris, a small tavern stands next to the Rue d'Enfer tollgate. Snow falls softly on the gray plane trees in the dim February dawn. The wintry stillness is punctuated by the clinking of glasses and faint laughter from inside the tavern.

Rousing the customs officers from their sleep, the street cleaners demand to pass through the gate. The barrier opens and they solemnly head to work, stamping their feet and rubbing their cold hands.

Mimi appears, trudging through the snow. She presses a handkerchief to her lips as she pauses to ask an officer directions to the tavern where she has heard Marcello is now working. At the inn, a maid agrees to fetch Marcello for her.

"Mimi!" exclaims the painter in surprise.

"I've found you at last."

"Musetta and I have been staying here for free. She sings for the patrons while I paint a mural for the innkeeper."

Mimi, her body racked by coughing, can barely stand. Marcello begs her to come inside out of the cold, but when she discovers Rodolfo is also staying at the inn, she tearfully refuses.

"Rodolfo is consumed by jealousy. At night when he thinks I'm sleeping, he even tries to spy on my dreams. So often he has told me our love is over, and last night he left."

"When two people are unhappy they shouldn't stay together," counsels Marcello regretfully. "Musetta and I live and let live, and so we are happy."

Mimi agrees with the painter and asks for his help in separating permanently from Rodolfo. Marcello promises to speak to him alone. At that moment, Rodolfo emerges from the tavern. While Marcello hurries to greet his friend, Mimi quickly hides.

"I'm miserable, Marcello. I want to leave Mimi," the unhappy poet declares. "She's just a flirt."

"You're not being honest."

A tortured melody rises as Rodolfo confesses the real problem. "You're right. I love her more than life itself, but she is seriously ill. The poor darling is doomed."

Mimi, listening from her hiding place, wonders fearfully, "Is it true? Am I really dying?"

Rodolfo tells Marcello that if Mimi continues to live in his unheated garret, it will only hasten her death. Just then, Mimi's cough betrays her presence, and Rodolfo

rushes to her side. Horrified that she may have heard his worries about her health, he tries to make light of them.

Marcello is brought back to his daily cares by the sound of Musetta's flirtatious laughter. He rushes into the tavern, tormented by suspicion.

Mimi bids a tearful goodbye to Rodolfo, telling him they should part as friends. Though they shake hands in farewell, neither can let go. At last they embrace, vowing to stay together until the return of spring.

Meanwhile, Marcello has chased Musetta out of the tavern and scolds her for flirting with one of the customers. As their voices rise in anger, Mimi and Rodolfo sing tenderly of springtime and its warming sun.

Musetta, threatening to leave Marcello, runs away through the snow. Marcello storms into the inn. Mimi and Rodolfo, however, have eyes only for each other and again they pledge to stay together until the flowers bloom.

Act IV

Months later, at work in the garret, Rodolfo and Marcello pause to discuss their former loves, Mimi and Musetta.

"I saw Musetta in a fancy carriage today," Rodolfo reveals, "and I asked her, how can you feel your heart beat under all that velvet?"

Marcello pretends to be amused, and quickly counters, "Guess who I saw the other day—Mimi, in a rich viscount's carriage, dressed like a queen."

Each knows the other's heart. In disgust, Rodolfo throws his pen to the floor, and Marcello tosses away his brush. Rising from his chair, the poet looks out of the window at the streets of Paris and sings a tender ode to Mimi, realizing that she will never come back to him. Marcello stares sadly at his painting and joins Rodolfo in a lament to their lost sweethearts.

At the close of their song, Schaunard and Colline enter the garret with dinner—a salted herring and a loaf of bread. Pretending it is the finest of delicacies, they pass the herring from person to person, singing its praises.

In the midst of their frivolity, Musetta bursts into the room and announces that Mimi is on the stairs, too weak to climb any further. Rodolfo rushes to her aid while Colline and Schaunard move the bed away from the window.

Rodolfo returns with Mimi, who is as pale as the white lace that adorns her dress and bonnet.

"Do you want me here with you?" she asks meekly.

"Always, my Mimi."

As Rodolfo helps her to the bed, Musetta explains: "I found the poor girl alone and helpless. She told me she wants to die near you, and so I brought her here."

Rodolfo removes Mimi's bonnet and covers her frail body with a blanket. She sits up slowly and smiles like a lost child who has found her way home.

"I'll get better now," she sings, and Rodolfo raises his voice in harmony with hers. Though he holds her tightly in his arms, Mimi shivers. "Will these cold hands of mine ever be warm? I wish I had a muff."

Musetta removes her earrings and begs Marcello to sell them to pay for a doctor. "I'm going with you to buy a muff for Mimi. It may be the poor girl's last request," she whispers as they leave the garret.

Colline suggests to Schaunard that they give the unhappy lovers a few private moments together, and the two leave as well.

Mimi reaches out for Rodolfo, and they embrace.

"Ah, my beautiful Mimi, as lovely as the dawn."

"You should have said the sunset," she murmurs sadly.

To cheer her, Rodolfo shows her the pink bonnet, his treasured keepsake, and they sing of their first meeting. Rodolfo is frightened when Mimi suddenly collapses in a fit of coughing, though she pretends that she feels fine.

The friends return. Musetta carries a white fur muff, and Marcello a bottle of medicine. Musetta gives the muff to Mimi, who places her hands inside the fur.

"The warmth will help . . . but I'm so tired," she sighs weakly.

Rodolfo turns away to hide his tears. Mimi's hand reaches out one final time before it drops suddenly to the bed, unseen by the poet.

While Musetta prays that Mimi will be spared, and Rodolfo draws the curtains to dim the sun's glare, Schaunard, suspecting the worst, tells Marcello that he fears Mimi has died. Marcello feels her pulse, and, confirming Schaunard's fear, drops to his knees. Rodolfo turns from the window and views the tragic scene.

"Courage, Rodolfo," says Marcello, embracing his friend.

Rodolfo's cry pierces the heart: "Mimi!"

Drawing close in their grief, Musetta throws her arms around Marcello. Tears stream down their cheeks as they watch Rodolfo hold Mimi's lifeless hand in his.

The curtain falls

Carmen

Escamillo

Don José

Micaela

CARMEN

Georges Bizet

Act I

A company of soldiers, stationed in Seville, lounges in the sun-drenched square outside their guardhouse, watching the passing crowd and joking among themselves. Morales, a young corporal, sees a pretty girl approach and is disappointed when he learns she is looking for another soldier, Don José.

"He'll be here soon. Come and wait inside," Morales and the soldiers coax. But she modestly declines, and disappears into the crowd.

The faint call of bugles and fifes announces the arrival of the new guard. Crossing a stone bridge, a troop of excited children marches merrily along like little soldiers to the beat of their playful song. Lieutenant Zuniga and Corporal Don José follow the children, leading their regiment into the square. The old guard and the relief guard salute each other and ceremoniously exchange places. Before Morales leaves with his men, he tells Don José of his charming visitor.

"That must be Micaela."

The soldiers, urchins, and townsfolk noisily leave the square and Lieutenant Zuniga, newly posted to Seville, questions Don José about life in the city.

"Tell me, are there pretty girls working in the cigarette factory over there?"

"I know nothing about those silly Andalusian women. My heart belongs to a girl from my village. But listen, it's noon and there's the factory bell. See for yourself."

Dozens of dark-haired factory girls saunter into the square to meet the young men who have gathered there. While their admirers serenade them, the girls puff lazily on their cigarettes, swaying gracefully to the languid music, their delicate hands undulating like spirals of smoke floating skyward. But the men are waiting for Carmen, the exotic gypsy girl, and when she enters the square she is at once the center of attention.

"When will you love us?" they all plead fervently.

"Who knows?" Carmen shrugs. "Maybe never. Maybe tomorrow. But certainly not today."

To the hypnotic rhythm of the Habañera, a Spanish folk song, Carmen lifts the hem of her skirt and dances toward her admirers.

"Love is a gypsy child. He has never heard of law. If you don't love me, I love you. If I love you, look out for yourself," she sings, glancing at José, who is fixing his musket and pays no attention to her. Carmen is attracted by his indifference.

"Friend, what are you doing?"

Don José, looking up from his work, finally notices her. Carmen pulls her dark curls away from her face to cool her burning cheeks, and, as a dissonant chord strikes, she takes an acacia flower from her bodice and tosses it at him.

José jumps to his feet, and everyone bursts into laughter. Carmen, pleased with her effect on him, runs into the factory, followed by the cigarette girls. The soldiers return to their barracks and the young men saunter away, leaving Don José alone in the square.

Slowly, as if in a trance, the young corporal stoops to pick up the flower that has landed at his feet.

"If there are witches, she's one for sure!"

He sees Micaela approaching and hides the flower in his jacket pocket.

"Your mother sent me with a letter for you and a little money to add to your pay and also. . . ."

"Go on," he insists kindly, taking her arm in his.

"She sends you a kiss which she made me promise to deliver." She kisses José on the forehead.

He looks into her eyes and sings of the happy, bygone days in his Basque village.

"Why, if you hadn't come just now, who knows into what demon's clutches I would have fallen. But my mother's kiss will protect me from harm."

José opens the letter and reads aloud: "'My son, I'm growing old. Perhaps, when you leave the service, you can come back to our village and get married. And there is no one better suited to be your wife than the bearer of this note.'"

Micaela is embarrassed and says goodbye, promising to return.

"Yes, Mama," José muses. "Soon I'll come back to you and our village and marry Micaela. As for that gypsy and her wicked flower. . . ."

He is about to throw the acacia blossom away when shrill cries erupt inside the tobacco factory.

The cigarette girls rush into the square screaming for help and are met by Lieutenant Zuniga. The girls, all chattering at once, explain that a fight has broken out between Carmen and Manuelita. Zuniga orders Don José to take some men inside to investigate, and, moments later, they lead Carmen out of the factory.

"They had an argument, and Carmen cut the other girl with a knife," José reports to the lieutenant.

"What have you to say?" Zuniga asks her.

Carmen regards him with an impudent smile and mockingly sings, "Cut me, burn me, I shall tell you nothing."

"It isn't songs I want. Give me an answer," cautions the lieutenant.

"I'm keeping my secret and keeping it well," she retorts.

Some of the girls shout, "Send her to prison!" Carmen lunges at them but is restrained by Zuniga.

"You're quick to attack," he concludes, motioning to Don José to tie her wrists together. "You'll sing your gypsy songs to the jailer, I'm afraid."

*　　*　　*

Inside the guardroom, Carmen complains, "The rope is too tight. My wrists hurt."

"I could loosen it," offers Don José.

"Why not let me escape?"

"Don't talk nonsense."

"You'll do as I wish. I know you took the flower, and by now it has worked its magic spell. You love me!"

Carmen leans against the wall and slides slowly down to the floor. Then, swaying from side to side, she sings a lilting song.

"On the outskirts of Seville at Lillas Pastia's tavern, I'll dance the seguidilla and drink manzanilla."

José is intrigued in spite of himself, and he moves his chair closer to her. Rising to her feet, Carmen dances for him, declaring that she'll bring the man she loves to Lillas's tavern.

"Carmen!" José cries softly, ensnared by her beauty and her promise.

"You're only a corporal, but that's good enough for a gypsy."

José can resist her charms no longer. He rushes to her and unties the rope. But as they embrace, the latch of the guardhouse door clicks loudly and footsteps are heard. Carmen puts her hands behind her back as José knots the cord loosely around her wrists. Lieutenant Zuniga has come with written orders for Carmen's imprisonment, and he instructs the corporal to escort her to jail.

As Don José leads her away, she whispers, "I'll push you as hard as I can. Let yourself fall—the rest is up to me."

Carmen strides past the staring crowd, humming the Habañera and smiling confidently. When they arrive at the bridge, she pushes José to his knees and escapes, fleeing over the bridge and out of sight.

Act II

It is late evening at Lillas Pastia's tavern, and the lanterns glow, casting a warm light on the revelers gathered there. Sitting at one of the tables with Carmen is Lieutenant Zuniga, who shows no interest in sending her back to prison. Two gypsies strum their guitars, girls dance, and the crowd claps and pounds the tables.

Carmen joins in the festivities, singing a gypsy song, and as the tempo quickens, she leaps to her feet. With her red and orange skirts swirling and her expressive hands undulating high above her head, she spins wildly to the rhythm of the music.

From afar, a chorus hails the arrival of Escamillo, the famous bullfighter, followed by a procession of his admirers. Toasting him with a glass of wine, Lieutenant Zuniga invites the toreador to join their party.

Escamillo accepts and sings the Toreador Song, extolling the pleasures of the fight, the joy of courage in the face of the bull, and the rewards of love that await the conqueror. Struck by Carmen's exotic beauty, he seems to sing for her ears alone. Carmen is fascinated by Escamillo, but she remains loyal to José.

Confident of his charm, Escamillo vows to wait patiently for Carmen to love him. Then, waving his hand to the cheering throng, the bullfighter takes his leave, joined by Zuniga, the soldiers, and his ardent fans.

At last, the inn is quiet. Lillas Pastia opens a side door and beckons two unshaven men with muddy boots into the room. They are Dancairo and Remendado, smugglers just returned from Gibraltar, who need Carmen and her friends Frasquita and Mercédès to help them bring their loot to the city. Carmen, who can usually be counted on, refuses to go. José has just been released from prison, and Carmen knows he will look for her at the tavern.

José is heard singing in the distance. With Mercédès and Frasquita on their arms, the smugglers leave Carmen alone, urging her to persuade her soldier to abandon his regiment and join their band.

Carmen rushes to the door to kiss José, and he declares that he would go to jail for her all over again if necessary.

"Your lieutenant was just here," Carmen teases, "and we danced for him and his soldiers. Are you jealous?"

"You know I am."

"Then I'll dance just for you."

Clicking a pair of castanets, Carmen hums a tune in time to the beat.

"Stop!" says José, hearing the faint cry of bugles. "Retreat is sounding. I must

return to the barracks for roll call."

Carmen is furious. "Run along then, yellow canary!" she taunts, accusing him of cowardice, and insisting that he doesn't love her.

This accusation is more than he can bear, and he pulls the wilted acacia from his pocket, singing of how its fragrance consoled him in his prison cell.

"You've captured my very soul, Carmen!"

She still insists he doesn't love her.

"If you did, you'd follow me into the mountains and ride like the wind away from the bugle calls, to freedom."

"Have pity, Carmen. Don't ask me to desert my regiment. I cannot!"

"Then I love you no more."

Saddened, yet unable to pay the terrible price of her love, José says goodbye to her forever. As he is about to leave, Zuniga returns to the tavern. Discovering José and Carmen together, he ridicules her for choosing a mere corporal over an officer, and orders José to leave. José refuses, and draws his sword.

Carmen screams for help. Dancairo and Remendado answer her call, followed by the gypsy girls. Disarming Zuniga, they point a pistol at his head and lead him away.

José knows he faces dishonor and prison after his mutinous act, and he reluctantly agrees to join Carmen and her friends. Singing victoriously, they assure him that true glory lies in a life of freedom.

Act III

In the dead of night, the smugglers follow a steep mountain path. They climb over the rocks to a clearing and, dropping their heavy bundles, settle down for a brief rest.

Dancairo and Remendado go ahead to see if the way into the city is clear, leaving José behind to guard the camp. He stares sullenly at Carmen.

"Don't you love me anymore?" he asks.

"Less and less every day," she replies spitefully. "I don't like being told what to do. I need to be free."

"If you ever leave me, Carmen, I'll. . . ."

"You'll what? Kill me?" she taunts.

Carmen turns her back on him and walks towards Mercédès and Frasquita, who are reading tarot cards. Mercédès sees a young, bold lover for herself. Frasquita discovers an old, wealthy husband in her future. Carmen decides to read her fortune, but the joyous music becomes ominous as she turns over the cards.

"Death! First me, then him. The cards tell the truth—there's no escape."

Dancairo and Remendado return from their scouting expedition with the news that three guards bar the route into town. Carmen, Mercédès, and Frasquita offer to flirt with the guards while the smugglers slip by, and they all set off, leaving José to watch the remaining goods.

José moves out of sight and the camp grows silent. Emerging from the shadows, Micaela, looking nervously about her, enters the camp. She sees José leaning against a rock, pointing a shotgun at the ridge below, and is about to call to him when he fires, nearly hitting another trespasser. It is Escamillo, the famous toreador. Micaela hides behind a rock as the bullfighter identifies himself.

"What do you want here?" demands José.

"I was rounding up bulls in the mountains and decided to pay a call on my latest love."

"What is her name?"

"Carmen. Her former boyfriend was a soldier who deserted for her, but I hear it's over now. Carmen's loves never last long."

José draws his knife.

"So, you're the man she once loved," mocks Escamillo, standing on guard, his dagger in hand.

José lunges at him, and they battle fiercely. Skillfully wielding his dagger, Escamillo points it at José's throat, offering to call off the fight. José refuses and the duel resumes. The bullfighter slips and falls, and José is about to stab his rival through the heart when Carmen and the smugglers return. They grab José's arm just in time to prevent the toreador's death.

Gallantly, Escamillo praises Carmen for saving his life, and offers to fight José again whenever he chooses. He tosses his jacket over his shoulder, and, looking at Carmen, invites whoever loves him to his next bullfight in Seville. As Escamillo leaves the camp, José warns Carmen to beware the wrath of a jilted lover.

The smugglers gather their belongings together. At that moment, Micaela makes herself known. She has come to plead with José to return to their village and to his mother, who is gravely ill.

"Go with her," scoffs Carmen. "You're not cut out for this life anyway."

"I'll go, Carmen, but we'll meet again." Dark music accompanies his threat.

José hears the faint voice of Escamillo, singing his proud Toreador Song. The dejected lover hesitates before leaving, turning round for a last look at Carmen, who stares into the distance after Escamillo.

Act IV

An excited crowd streams through the gates of the bullring. In the square outside the arena, merchants sell oranges, wine, fans, and cigarettes. Introduced by the spirited singing of the crowd, the procession of toreadors enters the square. The picadors on horseback lead the parade, followed by the great Escamillo. At his side, in a splendid dress and mantilla, is Carmen. Escamillo turns to her.

"If you love me, Carmen, you will soon be proud of your champion."

"I love you, and may death take me if I have ever loved any man more than you!"

Mercédès and Frasquita are waiting in the square for Carmen, and they warn her to be on guard—they have seen José hiding in the crowd.

"I'm not afraid. I'll stay here and speak to him," she says defiantly.

The mayor enters the bullring, followed by the procession. As the crowd thins, José appears. Carmen has not seen him since he left her to visit his dying mother.

"I was warned you were here and told to flee for my life."

"I'm not threatening you. I'm only begging you to forget the past and begin a new life with me far from this wretched place."

His plea is useless. Carmen declares that everything is finished between them. Unable to accept this, José sings of a love that can save them both.

"Whether I live or die, I won't give in to you," Carmen protests.

"Don't desert me now. I adore you more than life itself."

José's unrelenting demands suffocate Carmen.

"Free was I born, and free will I die!" she proclaims.

At that moment, cheers from inside the bullring draw Carmen's attention and she rushes toward the gate. José blocks her way, demanding that she run away with him. Carmen refuses, defiantly insisting she loves Escamillo.

"Kill me or let me go!" she cries as José's hold on her tightens.

The music is frantic and threatening. In a last attempt to convince José of the hopelessness of their love, Carmen throws a gold ring he once gave her into the dust.

José draws his knife and, holding Carmen in his arms, thrusts it into her heart.

Inside the bullring, the gay Toreador Song is sung in tribute to the victor, but outside the arena all is still. The spectators file out into the hot, silent square and, to their horror, discover the lifeless body of Carmen.

"Arrest me," José sobs, kneeling over her. "I've killed my beloved Carmen!"

The curtain falls

ACT IV

CARMEN

Act I

While Napoleon's army wages war across Europe, his Twenty-first Regiment can be found skirmishing in the mountains of the Swiss Tyrol. In a little glen on the outskirts of a village, the Tyrolean peasants take up position to fight off the approaching French troops. The village women gather near a small cottage and, singing softly, pray to heaven for protection.

Traveling home to her castle, the Marquise of Berkenfield is forced to take refuge in the village with her steward, Hortensius. In a quavering voice, the exasperated Marquise gives vent to her feelings.

"How dreadful are the times of war for those of rank and station. Such discomfort and aggravation! Life has no real style anymore."

A peasant, keeping watch on the mountainside, suddenly exclaims, "Have no fear! The French are retreating!"

Everyone rejoices. The Marquise decides to remain in the village rather than continue her dangerous journey and sends Hortensius to watch over her carriage. While she chatters to the villagers, Sulpice, the burly sergeant of the French grenadiers, arrives. The mere sight of him sends the terrified villagers scurrying away, and the Marquise takes refuge in the nearby cottage.

Sulpice, amazed at such cowardice, declares that the regiment wants to make peace. At that moment, a lovely soprano is heard—the voice of Marie, the daughter of the regiment.

A pretty girl in a grenadier's uniform approaches Sulpice, one of her many adopted fathers. A drum and a canteen are strapped around her neck. Taking great pride in her military upbringing, Marie sings of her childhood in the regiment, raised by a loving and attentive family of fathers.

"In the hubbub of war, I was born. The thunder of battle was my lullaby. Country and victory, that's my motto!"

"What a lucky day it was when Providence delivered you, an orphan, into my arms," reminisces Sulpice.

"My loving fathers happily carried me on their backs. And now that I am grown, I march into the field of honor as your canteen girl."

Together, they sing of their love of battle. Marie deftly plays her drum as her voice rings out, "Rataplan! Rataplan!"

When their duet ends, Sulpice decides to question his daughter on a delicate matter.

"Why have you been avoiding us recently? You've been seen spending time with a stranger, haven't you?"

No sooner does Marie confess that she has fallen in love with a Tyrolean man than the grenadiers of the Twenty-first arrive, dragging and pushing a young prisoner.

"Goodness gracious, it's my Tonio!" she cries.

The young Tyrolese has wandered into the camp in search of Marie and been arrested for spying. Striking a dramatic pose, Marie begs the troops to spare him and explains how he saved her life.

"Had it not been for Tonio, I would have fallen to my death from a precipice. Now, do you still sentence him to death for spying?"

At last, the soldiers recognize their error. They gather around a rum keg, fill their mugs, and toast their daughter's savior. Sulpice calls for Marie to lead them in the regimental song, and she dances down a line of proud grenadiers, singing their praises.

When a drum announces roll call, Sulpice commands his men to take their positions.

"You, my boy, file in!" he barks at Tonio.

"He's my prisoner. I'll answer for him," intercedes Marie.

Sulpice insists that the young Tyrolese follow the grenadiers back to camp. Tonio obeys, marching off with the regiment, but the angry Marie stays behind. Moments later, Tonio returns.

"I fled at the first crossroad. The sergeant yelled like a madman."

"My father," nods Marie.

"No, I mean the other sergeant."

"My father."

"No, no, the old one."

"He's my father too."

"Honestly, Marie. Have you got an entire regiment for a father?" he jokes.

"That's right. The regiment is my father by adoption."

Marie asks him why he risked his life to see her again. Gazing into her eyes, Tonio declares his love, telling how he braved enemy fire to find her, and Marie in turn admits her love for him. As they realize their feelings are shared, they burst into a cheerful duet, swearing to be true to one another forever.

Sulpice returns to discover the couple embracing, but they take no notice of him and wander off together. The Marquise comes out of the cottage and addresses Sulpice.

"I wish to return home, but the mountains are full of soldiers. Can you offer me safe conduct to my château?"

"What is the name of your castle?"

THE DAUGHTER OF THE REGIMENT

"Berkenfield—like my own name."

Sulpice recognizes the name and recalls its connection to that of a certain Captain Robert. At the mention of Captain Robert, the Marquise nearly faints.

"Did you know him?" asks Sulpice.

Blushing, the Marquise stammers, "Not I but, er . . . my sister, yes, it was my late sister."

The Marquise tells the sergeant that a daughter was born of the marriage of Captain Robert and her sister.

"When the captain died, I was to be the child's guardian, but the old servant entrusted with her care also died." The Marquise reveals that her niece was lost and may even be dead.

"No, not dead!" rejoices Sulpice. "Saved and adopted by us, the Twenty-first."

Amazed to discover that her niece is alive, the Marquise turns to find Marie entering the glen.

"Who's that lady?" the girl asks rudely.

"Shh, Marie! This is your aunt."

"My aunt! *Sacré bleu!*"

Shocked by her language and manners, the Marquise decides to remove Marie from the care of her guardians. At first Marie refuses to go, but on learning of her real father and of his dying wish that she be raised by the Marquise, the reluctant girl agrees. Sulpice comforts her and together they leave the glen to prepare for Marie's departure.

A drum roll summons the regiment and the soldiers hasten to take their positions, singing the praises of war and victory. Tonio approaches, dressed in a French uniform. Having learned that only a grenadier may seek Marie's hand in marriage, Tonio has enlisted in the Twenty-first.

"Oh, my friends, love has turned my head. To win Marie, I have chosen this new calling."

Begging her fathers to hear his suit, Tonio adds: "It is for you to decide whether I am to become her husband."

"Our daughter must make a better match," they chorus. "She must marry a Frenchman. That's a father's wish."

"But your daughter loves me!"

The soldiers carefully consider this development and finally consent to the match. Overjoyed, Tonio sings of his good fortune, swearing again that Marie returns his love.

"She cannot be married to anyone!" declares Sulpice, rejoining his men. "Her aunt has claimed her, and they leave today for Berkenfield."

Tonio's hopes are crushed. Accompanied by the Marquise, Marie enters the glen and confirms Sulpice's amazing tale. To a melancholy tune, she grieves over her imminent departure and bids a heartbreaking goodbye to her fathers. Tonio, Sulpice, and the soldiers join her song, barely able to hold back their tears.

"I shall follow you," declares Tonio.

"Didn't you enlist?" Sulpice reminds him.

Marie notices his uniform for the first time and is astounded by this ironic twist.

"I must lose him just when I might be married to him!" she laments.

Though the Marquise is sympathetic, she nevertheless insists that Marie return with her to Berkenfield. Marie and Tonio pledge to love each other forever, and, for the second time in their brief courtship, they bid farewell.

Act II

Several weeks have passed. The Marquise has now arranged an advantageous marriage for Marie and has asked Sergeant Sulpice to help convince her niece.

"Thanks to my pains, Marie has almost become a lady. I have promised her to one of the greatest men in Germany, the Duke of Krakenthorp. His mother arrives this evening to sign the marriage contract."

"A canteen girl to be a duchess?" marvels Sulpice.

When Marie enters the salon, her aunt hushes Sulpice. Marie's military uniform has been replaced by a satin gown and the drum strap around her neck by a string of pearls.

"Come here my child," beckons the Marquise, seating herself at the piano for Marie's lesson. "When the old duchess hears your beautiful voice, she'll have no qualms about your upbringing."

With great flourish but not much skill, the Marquise strikes the keys. Marie begins in earnest, but she is unable to follow the languid pace of the aria her aunt has chosen. When Sulpice interjects "Rataplan! Rataplan!" Marie soon finds herself singing the regimental song.

"Goodness, what's that?" asks the horrified Marquise.

Marie tries again, trilling elegantly to her aunt's music. When she hesitates over a line, the sergeant prompts her with a phrase from the military song. This immediately sets her off on the wrong track and she breaks into the regimental roundelay.

"Rataplan plan plan, forward march!" sing Marie and Sulpice, holding hands and spinning around the room in delight. Against her better judgment, the Marquise joins

in the fun, dancing merrily till she collapses on the piano bench.

"You must control your enthusiasm, niece, if you are to be a duchess," the Marquise observes, rising to her feet and exiting on Sulpice's arm.

Left alone, Marie gives voice to her unhappiness. "What use are beauty and grace when my beloved is not here? Where are you, my dearest Tonio?"

Without her sweetheart there to claim her, Marie resigns herself to accepting the hateful marriage contract. But just then, the distant strains of a military march announce the arrival of the Twenty-first.

"Hurray for France, for those happy times, for hope, and for my love!" she cries.

The grenadiers burst into the salon and surround their darling Marie. Hearing the commotion, Sulpice returns and is delighted to find his regiment. And finally, Tonio, promoted for gallantry to the rank of lieutenant, races into the room and sweeps Marie into his arms.

Hortensius, alarmed by the noise in the salon, comes in to investigate. Despite his disapproval, Marie orders him to pour her aunt's finest wine and serve it to the regiment. As he stamps off, the soldiers follow him to the cellar, leaving Tonio, Marie, and Sulpice to a private celebration.

The Marquise enters the salon and demands an explanation. Tonio avows his love for Marie, describing how he has sacrificed home and country for her.

"My niece is promised, sir. The contract is to be signed in an hour and I must ask you to leave at once."

Heartbroken, Marie goes to her room while Tonio leaves through another door. Sulpice, at the Marquise's insistence, remains behind.

"Sir, I must throw myself upon your mercy," she implores, wringing her hands nervously.

The Marquise confesses that Marie is, in fact, her own daughter. Separated by war, Captain Robert was unable to return to marry the Marquise before his death.

"I had to conceal Marie's birth, but now I have an opportunity to set things right. The marriage to Krakenthorp will confer a name and title upon her and will allow me to leave her all I possess."

She begs Sulpice to persuade Marie to marry the duke. Sympathizing with the Marquise's plight, he agrees.

Hortensius announces the arrival of the guests. To a stately minuet, the Duchess and her entourage enter.

"Your Grace, my niece and I have been impatiently awaiting your arrival," declares the Marquise.

THE DAUGHTER OF THE REGIMENT

The haughty dowager looks around the room, noting Marie's absence with disapproval. Once the Duchess is seated, the notary enters, bearing the marriage contract.

"Is everyone present?" he asks.

"Everyone but the bride!" snaps the Duchess.

Suddenly, to the Marquise's relief, Marie rushes into the room, followed by Sulpice. She throws herself into the Marquise's arms and murmurs, "My mother!"

"My child," whispers the Marquise lovingly.

Having learned the story of her birth from Sulpice, Marie's only wish is to make her mother happy. She takes a pen from the notary and is about to sign the document when loud voices and the sound of trampling feet interrupt.

"Follow me!" cries Tonio, leading the regiment into the salon. Singing of their mission to rescue Marie from further suffering, the soldiers claim her as their daughter.

The Duchess and the guests demand an explanation. The men reveal that Marie is their canteen girl, the daughter of the regiment. Shock waves ripple through the crowd as Marie steps forward.

"When Fate, in the middle of the war, threw me into their arms, they welcomed me and guided my first steps. Can my heart forget them, when I'm only alive today through their kindness?"

The guests are impressed by her words and think her more charming than before. The Duchess, equally impressed, indicates her approval. To Tonio's horror, Marie still intends to sign the contract, but this time it is the Marquise who stops the proceedings.

"My child, so much unhappiness and all for me. Away with pride! I give you the husband of your choice."

Amidst the approving murmurs of the company, Tonio and Marie join hands. Singing merrily, everyone rejoices at this happy conclusion as the voices of Marie and Tonio soar above the rest.

The curtain falls

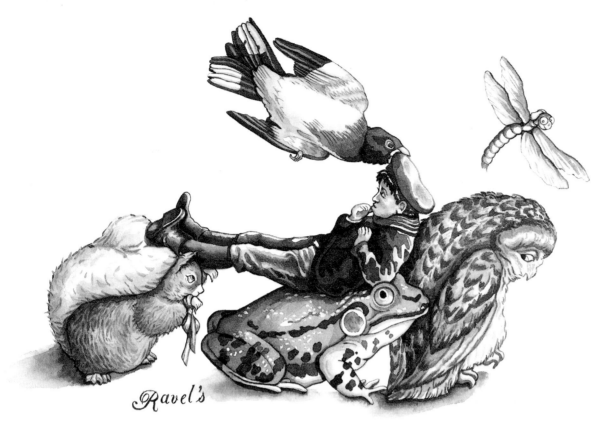

Ravel's
L'Enfant et les Sortilèges

In a large room overlooking a garden, a little boy of six or seven sits in front of his schoolbooks, surrounded by familiar things—the grandfather clock, the squirrel in its cage, the cat. The boy stares at his homework, but he would rather misbehave than study.

The door opens and his mother enters, carrying his tea on a tray.

"Has Mother's boy been good and finished his lesson?"

She notices the ink-stained carpet under his feet and the unfinished lesson on the table, and she scolds him for his laziness. When she asks for an apology, the unrepentant boy sticks out his tongue.

"Here's food for a naughty child: tea without sugar and dry bread. You'll stay alone till dinner and think about how sad you've made me."

The furious child throws a temper tantrum. He knocks his cup and teapot off the table, opens the cage and pricks the squirrel with his pen, pulls the cat's tail, and stirs up the fire with a poker, sending a cloud of ash and smoke into the room.

"Hurrah!" he shouts, stabbing the little shepherds and shepherdesses on the wallpaper with the poker. Large sections tear away from the wall.

"Hurrah!" he howls again, swinging on the pendulum of the grandfather clock.

But he isn't satisfied till he rips his books to pieces.

"No more lessons! No more homework! I'm free—naughty and free!"

The wicked boy flops into an easy chair, but it collapses beneath him. Then, to his utter amazement, the Armchair comes magically to life and creeps away like a giant toad.

"Now we're forever rid of this child with his horrid heels," the Armchair says to a little Louis XV Chair.

In chorus, Bench, Sofa, Ottoman, and Wicker Chair agree: "No more of that child!"

Suddenly, Grandfather Clock chimes in, "I no longer know the time. He has broken my pendulum!"

Grandfather Clock careens about the room and turns his face to the wall to hide his shame.

The child can barely catch his breath, so astonished is he. The cracked black Wedgwood Teapot rights himself and asks the chipped Chinese Cup to dance to a jazzy foxtrot. Then, brandishing his fists, he growls at the boy, "I box you, sir, I marmalade you!"

The setting sun casts a pink glow into the enchanted room. Fearfully, the child approaches the fireplace to warm himself, but Fire leaps out and chases the boy around the room.

"I warm the good but burn the bad! Foolhardy little savage, you've insulted all the friendly household gods!" trills Fire.

Cinder follows in her footsteps, gently extinguishing the dancing flames. Shadows haunt the walls and ceiling of the room and the child whispers, "I'm afraid."

Shy giggles reach his ears. The characters from the torn wallpaper spring to life, and the Shepherds and Shepherdesses mourn the loss of their nursery-tale existence.

"Ungrateful child, who has slept while our blue dog, violet goat, and pink sheep kept watch over him!"

Weeping, the boy lies on the floor, his face buried in the pages from a torn and abandoned storybook. A golden-haired Princess rises from a page—the heroine of a fairy tale.

"Help! Sleep and night want to take me!" she cries as the floor opens beneath her and she slips away.

L'Enfant et les Sortilèges

In a small, clear voice the child grieves for the little Princess. In vain, he leafs through the scattered pages to find the end of the story, and in frustration kicks his arithmetic book. Angry voices screech at him and Numbers fly out from between the pages, hovering menacingly over his head. A Little Old Man emerges from the book and, tapping a ruler on the floor in time to the music, reels off mathematical problems.

"*Mon Dieu!* It's Father Arithmetic," cries the horrified child.

In a falsetto voice, the Little Old Man chants the arithmetic tables at an ever-increasing rate, while the Numbers force the child into a frenzied dance. When at last his tormentors disappear, the dizzy boy falls to the floor.

The moon rises, illuminating a wall of the room. The Black Cat creeps out from under the Armchair and casts a shadow over the child's head.

"Is it you, kitty? You can speak too, no doubt?"

Black Cat hisses. When a White Cat perches on the window sill, Black Cat leaves the boy to dance with her. Purring flirtatiously, they leap into the garden. The child is about to follow them through the open window, when the walls of the room dissolve and he is transported into the moonlit garden.

Mysterious music rises, mimicking the buzzing of insects, the muttering of frogs, the screech of owls, and the song of nightingales. The boy tries to lean against his favorite tree, but it groans, "My wound, it's still bleeding sap from the knife cut you made in my side!"

Dragonflies flutter overhead. One alights beside the boy, demanding to know the whereabouts of his companion. Ashamed, the child reveals that the insect is pinned to his bedroom wall.

A Bat scolds the boy for killing his mate with a stick the night before.

"The nest full . . . little ones . . . with no mother."

Aghast at the results of his cruelty, the child begs for forgiveness. A Frog hops onto the boy's lap and rests there. From a high branch a Squirrel looks down and warns the Frog to stay away from such a dangerous child—a boy who imprisons squirrels in cages and takes away their freedom. Other Squirrels jump down from the trees and dance in the moonlight. Bats swoop, Moths flutter, Cats play, Frogs leap, and the child suddenly realizes that he is alone and forgotten.

"They love each other. They're happy, but I'm alone. Mama!"

The boy's cry upsets the delicate balance in the garden. Enraged, the trees and animals surround the child, and, in a thundering chorus, they list their grievances. Then, clawing and scratching, they attack him. In the confusion, the animals turn on one another, and the injured boy lies forgotten in a corner. Near him, a Squirrel licks his bleeding paw. The child takes a ribbon from his neck, binds up the wound, and then collapses. Awestruck, his adversaries gather round him.

"He has dressed the wound . . . he is wise," observes an Owl.

"He has stopped the bleeding . . . he is good," comments a Nightingale.

With this kind act, the boy proves that he is capable of good, and the animals decide to make amends. As the Dragonflies fan him with their wings, the other animals lift the child and carry him to the house.

"Let's take him back to his nest. That's where we'll find help for the wounded child!"

They imitate his cry of "Mama!" and a light appears in the window. The animals, though reluctant to leave their new friend, bound away.

Radiant in the moonlight, the child holds out his arms and calls, "Mama!"

The curtain falls

Act I

Gabriel von Eisenstein's opulent Belle Epoque salon appears to be empty. Only the voice of Alfred, a professional tenor, can be heard through the open terrace doors, serenading Rosalinde, the mistress of the house. Alfred, an old flame of Rosalinde's, begs her to love him once again.

Adele, Rosalinde's chambermaid, runs merrily into the room holding a feather duster in one hand and a letter in the other. Her sister Ida, a ballerina, has sent word of a fancy dinner dance to be held that evening at the home of the eccentric Russian millionaire, Prince Orlofsky. Urging Adele to borrow one of her mistress's gowns, Ida invites her to the ball. Adele's hopes are dashed, however, when she realizes that she has housework to do and little chance of getting the evening off.

As she dusts the furniture, Alfred's song is heard again and she runs into the garden to investigate. At that moment Rosalinde, wearing a satin dressing gown over layers of silk petticoats, descends the staircase. She frantically paces about, then collapses on the divan, pressing her temples.

"Imagine, Alfred comes back now when I'm a married woman. What a scandal! Oh, my poor head!"

Adele returns from the terrace, spies her mistress, and bursts into a high-pitched wail.

"My sick auntie desperately needs me. I must have the night off."

"Impossible!"

Rosalinde reminds Adele that she is needed at home, since Herr von Eisenstein has to leave that evening to serve a short prison sentence for hitting a police officer over the head. Adele storms up the stairs, bemoaning the fate that made her a housemaid.

Alfred sneaks into the room through the terrace doors and kisses Rosalinde on the nape of the neck. The startled woman leaps to her feet and begs Alfred to leave at once.

"I'm married now," she protests.

"I don't mind. Everyone knows your husband is in jail."

"Not yet! He's coming home at any moment to pack his toothbrush."

Alfred refuses to leave until Rosalinde has reluctantly promised to see him later. No sooner does he go than Gabriel von Eisenstein bursts through the door, followed by his bungling attorney, Dr. Blind. They have returned from a frustrating day in court and are quarreling. Rosalinde offers a tender show of concern as her husband rails bitterly against the legal profession.

"Lawyers! First they butter you up, then they sell you out. Now I'm in even worse trouble."

As Eisenstein and Blind sputter and screech abuse at one another in a frantic duet, Rosalinde joins in, ordering the lawyer to leave. Dr. Blind finally hobbles off, leaving Frau von Eisenstein to soothe her suffering husband.

"Five days—that's all," she sings sweetly, helping Gabriel into his dressing gown and guiding him to an armchair.

"Now it's eight, thanks to my lawyer!"

The strain of his impending prison term has given Herr von Eisenstein a tremendous appetite, and he orders a lavish farewell banquet. He then asks his wife to find his oldest and shabbiest suit—appropriate attire for a jail cell. As she is about to climb the stairs to her husband's dressing room, Dr. Falke, Eisenstein's close friend, arrives. Rosalinde begs him to cheer up the sullen Gabriel, and goes to fetch the clothes.

"What brings you here?" asks Eisenstein glumly.

"The most beautiful ladies of Vienna await you at Prince Orlofsky's villa tonight."

"But my jail sentence starts this evening."

"A mere trifle. You can't be expected to miss the lovely ballerinas at Orlofsky's party."

His interest aroused, Gabriel pulls out his bejeweled pocket watch to see how much time he has left as a free man.

"Ah, your irresistible bait for catching the ladies," observes Dr. Falke. "You promise that watch to every woman you fancy."

"But no one has gained it yet."

To the jolly strains of a polka, Dr. Falke encourages his friend to come to Orlofsky's villa. He knows that Eisenstein can't resist a party or a beautiful woman.

"Your wife will assume you're in jail and, in her distress, will retire for the evening. We'll sneak off to the party, where I'll introduce you as a Frenchman, the Marquis Renard. No one will recognize you and you won't be arrested."

The two friends agree that the party will be a perfect tonic for Eisenstein, boosting his spirits before his jail term. When Rosalinde descends the stairs carrying a shabby hat and coat, she finds the men laughing and dancing about the room.

Dr. Falke notices the old clothes draped over Rosalinde's arm and realizes his friend cannot wear rags to Orlofsky's ball.

"If you dress your husband like a bandit, Rosalinde, they may throw him in with the real criminals."

Aghast at the prospect, Rosalinde nods in agreement as Dr. Falke bids farewell.

Gabriel removes his dressing gown and announces that he now intends to go to jail in full evening dress.

"I'll wear my top hat and tails as a protest," he chortles, bounding up the stairs and into his dressing room.

After marveling at her husband's high spirits, Rosalinde's thoughts turn to Alfred's promised visit. When Adele enters with the supper tray, Rosalinde realizes she must be alone when Alfred returns and informs Adele that she may have the night off after all. Adele kisses her mistress's hand in thanks as Eisenstein, splendidly attired, skips down the stairs. He waves to his wife and is nearly through the door when Rosalinde stops him.

"But your supper is on the table."

"I've decided to fast," he answers guiltily.

Wishing to appear grief-stricken, though now secretly looking forward to Alfred's arrival, Rosalinde bursts into a mournful song. Gabriel makes a gallant show of comforting her, while Adele, suspecting that both are insincere, watches with amusement.

"Oh Lord, how moved I am," they sing in unison, burying their bowed heads in their hands. But anticipation of the evening ahead makes all three giddy, and the tempo speeds up till they are kicking their heels together and singing with glee. Donning his evening cape, silk scarf, and top hat, Gabriel bows majestically and the trio bid a touching farewell. But they can't help themselves and again break into their merry song as the master of the house disappears and Adele leaves for the evening.

Alfred steals in through the terrace doors and discovers a wonderful meal laid out on the table. He makes himself at home, removing his coat and slipping on Eisenstein's dressing gown, which he finds draped over the divan.

"Aren't you looking forward to tonight?" he asks, sitting down and drawing Rosalinde to his knee. "Happiness is forgetting what you can't change anyway. Drink with me! Sing with me! Love me now, that's all I ask."

Despite her protests, she is carried away by his rhapsodic song and joins him in a beautiful duet. As Alfred is about to kiss her, they hear a loud commotion at the front door. Rosalinde assumes it is Gabriel and begs Alfred to leave. The tenor, however, stretches out on the divan with a glass of wine.

Frank, the prison warden, in full evening dress, enters the room. "Madame, before I go out tonight, I will personally escort your husband to jail."

Alfred continues to drink wine and hum his love song. The warden naturally assumes that the gentleman is Gabriel.

"My carriage is waiting," he tells Alfred. "I hope you won't put up any resistance, Herr von Eisenstein."

Blushing, Rosalinde whispers to Alfred that he must pretend to be her husband for the sake of her honor. And, in an effort to convince the suspicious warden that the man in question is truly married to her, she sits on Alfred's lap.

"If I have to do time for your husband, then at least I'll do his kissing for him too," Alfred whispers in her ear, taking advantage of this opportunity.

The warden assures Alfred that going to jail is as pleasant as being a bird in a cage. When Frank finally pulls the lovestruck tenor out through the door, Rosalinde collapses, exhausted, on the divan.

Act II

Prince Orlofsky's guests sweep into the ballroom of his famous villa. Singing merrily, they all agree: "This is the party of the year!"

Adele wanders into the ballroom wearing one of Rosalinde's most beautiful gowns. Her sister, Ida, is astonished to see her.

"Who invited you?" she asks.

"I received your letter asking me to come."

"It wasn't my letter—someone's played a trick on you. I'll have to introduce you as an actress."

Accompanied by Dr. Falke, Prince Orlofsky enters with a bored expression on his haughty young face.

"I can't laugh anymore, everything is so dull," he complains.

"You shall laugh tonight," promises the doctor. "I've gone to great lengths to prepare a little domestic comedy for you. It's called *The Revenge of the Bat*."

Orlofsky's face brightens when Falke identifies Adele as one of his principal "performers." Adele is introduced to the prince by her sister as Frau Olga, the actress, and Orlofsky generously sends the girls off to the gaming tables with the contents of his wallet.

Falke reveals to Orlofsky that Olga is really Adele, a chambermaid employed by the leading man in the comedy he has arranged. As if on cue, the Marquis Renard is announced and Gabriel enters. Orlofsky, intrigued by the unfolding drama, offers the marquis a glass of vodka, insisting that they drink together.

In a nonchalant, aristocratic voice, Orlofsky sings, "I love my guests to have a good time. Whatever they do is fine. But they must drink copiously or risk being hit over the head with a bottle of vodka. *Chacun à son goût.*"

Adele returns with Ida from their gambling and is shocked to see her employer.

"You bear a striking resemblance to my chambermaid," declares Gabriel, in a voice loud enough to be overheard by all.

To a lyrical waltz, Adele defends her features as classic and elegant, and Eisenstein squirms as the crowd laughs with her. Marveling that he could confuse her with a housemaid, she addresses him knowingly as Mein Herr Marquis, increasing his discomfort.

But the fun is just beginning. The Chevalier Chagrin is announced and in walks Frank, the prison warden. After revealing Chagrin's true identity to Orlofsky, Falke introduces the chevalier to the marquis as a fellow Frenchman. Forced to speak in French, neither gentleman can construct a single comprehensible sentence. They are rescued from their foolishness by Falke, who has an announcement to make.

"The prince expects a special guest—a well-known Hungarian countess whose presence must be kept a secret. She'll be wearing a mask to conceal her identity."

The crowd murmurs with excitement, but Eisenstein is the most curious of all.

"I imagine the woman is married," he says eagerly.

"Yes, to a jealous old fool," replies Falke.

When the prince proposes a tour of his villa, everyone follows—everyone except Dr. Falke, who waits for his leading lady, the countess.

In a few moments an exotic beauty, wearing a black mask trimmed with rhinestones and feathers, enters the empty ballroom.

"I never would have recognized you in the costume I sent!" Falke says to the mysterious stranger, who is none other than Rosalinde.

Falke has informed her in a note that Gabriel intends to forgo prison in favor of an evening's frolic. Rosalinde peers into the garden and discovers not only her husband, but her chambermaid as well. Irate, Rosalinde is about to confront the maid when Eisenstein comes in from the garden.

Introducing himself, Gabriel dangles his little watch before Rosalinde's eyes, trying to persuade her to remove the mask. Rosalinde maintains her disguise and, in an exaggerated Hungarian accent, she flirts with the marquis. The couple sing a lively duet in which Eisenstein extols the countess's virtues, while Rosalinde, singing to herself, plots her revenge.

"Won't you count my heartbeats on your lovely watch?" she asks breathlessly.

Eisenstein draws close, hands Rosalinde the watch, and places his ear to her heart. After they count the beats, the countess pockets the watch, thanking the marquis for his charming gift.

"She didn't fall into my trap. She's had the last laugh!" he curses in disbelief.

Rosalinde sings jubilantly; and the partygoers, hearing her lovely soprano, pour into the ballroom.

Bold and impetuous in her disguise as an actress, Adele demands that the countess remove her mask. "How do we know you're a real Hungarian?"

Even the revelers clamor for proof. Rosalinde accepts the challenge and sings a heartfelt Czardas in praise of Hungary. The partygoers roar their approval and Eisenstein is more smitten than ever.

At last dinner is announced and the guests take their seats in the dining hall. Orlofsky suggests that Falke amuse everyone with the story of the bat, but Eisenstein insists that he is the only one who can do justice to the tale.

"Two years ago the doctor and I attended a masked ball. I dressed as a butterfly, Falke as a *Fledermaus*—a bat. After an evening of revelry, I intentionally left him in the park. He was thoroughly intoxicated, and had to lie in the grass, enduring the jeers and taunts of the passers-by. Since then, everyone calls him Dr. Fledermaus."

"And did he take his revenge?" asks Orlofsky with a curious smile on his face.

"Since then, I've always been on my guard."

Anticipating a hilarious outcome to what he knows will soon be Falke's revenge, Orlofsky, in high spirits, raises his glass and sings, "Long live champagne, the King!" The guests gulp their champagne and join in the joyful song.

As dawn approaches, the prince proposes a waltz, and the lyrical strains of the Viennese music envelop the senses. While everyone dances, the chevalier and the marquis pledge eternal friendship.

"How touching it will be when they meet again in jail," giggle Falke and Rosalinde.

The clock chimes six, and Renard and Chagrin call for their hats, each realizing that he is long overdue at the prison. Arm in arm they bid the party goodnight and dance tipsily out of the door.

Orlofsky, wishing he could be present when the warden meets his prisoner, laughs uproariously at the inevitable outcome of the bat's revenge.

Act III

Gulping plum brandy, Frosch, the jailer, yells for quiet. Alfred, locked in cell number twelve, is loudly singing the *Miserere* from *Trovatore*.

"This isn't an opera house! This is a respectable place," Frosch mutters as he slowly climbs the staircase to the cell.

As the jailer disappears through the door of the upper landing, Frank, the prison warden, staggers into the jailhouse. With great difficulty, he puts on his uniform and then sits down at his desk, lights a cigar, picks up his newspaper, and immediately falls asleep. Frosch descends the staircase, steals the cigar from Frank's mouth, and wakes him for the morning report.

"The prisoner in number twelve is asking for his lawyer."

"Call him then, you idiot!" bellows Frank.

When the doorbell rings, Frosch staggers to the door and, flinging it wide, announces the arrival of Adele and her sister. Fluttering her eyelashes at Frank, Adele confesses that she is not an actress at all but is really Herr von Eisenstein's chambermaid.

"I can't go back to my old job, so I've come to ask you to be my patron. I belong on the stage, not in the kitchen."

Frosch interrupts to announce another visitor—the Marquis Renard. Adele and Ida are shown to an empty cell.

When Eisenstein discovers the chevalier at the prison, he is amazed. Frank confesses that he is really the warden, and Eisenstein reveals his own true identity.

"Impossible!" scoffs Frank. "I arrested Eisenstein last night in the midst of an intimate supper with his wife. They were a cozy pair in their dressing gowns."

Eisenstein is baffled and insists on speaking to the man who is masquerading as himself.

"I'm sorry, you need a permit," Frank says, climbing the stairs to check on Adele and Ida.

The door flies open, and Dr. Blind walks into the jailhouse. "You summoned me?"

"I didn't call you," responds Eisenstein in a fury. But he is struck with an idea. He drags Dr. Blind to the cloakroom and disguises himself in the attorney's clothes and wig.

Alfred, still wearing Gabriel's dressing gown, is brought from his cell by Frosch to

wait for Dr. Blind. When the jailer leaves, Rosalinde runs into the room. Alfred serenades her as usual.

"Can't you be serious?" she pleads nervously. "My husband will be here at any minute. He mustn't find you in his dressing gown!"

Alfred assures her that he has called her lawyer to help them. Eisenstein, disguised as Dr. Blind, walks through the door, hiding his head behind his briefcase.

"Explain why I should defend you."

Alfred says that he was arrested by mistake, while dining with Rosalinde.

"You deserved it, you scoundrel!" yelps Gabriel.

Rosalinde assures him that nothing scandalous took place.

"But I depend on your discretion, because my husband might think otherwise."

"And he'd be right!"

"You seem to have more sympathy for my husband than for me, but he's a scoundrel. All last night, he was the life of the party, shamelessly flirting with young dancing girls."

Singing with great intensity, she cries, "I'll scratch his eyes out, then I'll get a divorce."

When Alfred asks "Dr. Blind" how they can teach Eisenstein a lesson, the impostor is enraged. Shedding his hat, wig, and cloak, he screams for revenge and chases Alfred around the room. Rosalinde catches her husband's coattails, dangles the watch, and in a Hungarian accent asks, "Would you like to count my heartbeats, Marquis?"

His duplicity discovered, Gabriel admits, "I'm a fool!"

"And now that you're here, you can serve the rest of your sentence," says Alfred.

Frank enters the room, and demands to know who is the real Eisenstein. Gabriel denies his true identity just as Adele and Ida, escorted by Frosch, descend the stairs.

"My mistress and her husband!" Adele shrieks, pointing to Rosalinde and Eisenstein.

Before Frank can throw Gabriel in a cell, Falke, Orlofsky, and the entire party crowd into the jailhouse. The room overflows with drunken revelers who cry, "Oh, Bat, let your victim go!"

"What's this?" asks Eisenstein.

"*The Revenge of the Bat!*" retorts Falke, admitting that he cooked up the elaborate scheme to get even with his friend.

Singing merrily, all those assembled acknowledge their roles. Even Alfred doesn't have the heart to destroy a husband's happiness, and he pretends his liaison with Rosalinde was all part of the plan.

"What about me?" whines Adele.

When Frank offers to find her a job in the theater, and Orlofsky promises to pay for her debut, everyone is happy save Rosalinde.

"Pardon your Gabriel," cajoles her husband. "It wasn't my fault I strayed. The cause of all this was champagne!"

Suddenly gay, Rosalinde's beautiful voice rings out in a toast to champagne, and she forgives her husband. She kisses him while the revelers dance merrily, exulting in the healing powers of King Champagne.

The curtain falls

Act I

On the edge of a great forest dwell Peter, a poor broommaker, his wife, Gertrude, and their two children, Hansel and Gretel. The family's cottage is sparsely furnished: a table, some wooden chairs, and hay in the sleeping loft are the only comforts they can afford. As a gentle melody envelops the little cottage, Gretel mends a stocking and Hansel, seated upstairs in the loft, makes brooms. It's nearly suppertime, but there's nothing to eat and no sign of their parents who left for town at dawn to sell brooms.

Putting down her knitting to stroke the cat, Gretel sings a nursery rhyme: "Susie, little Susie, now listen with care. The geese are running barefoot, they've no shoes to wear."

"Goosy, goosy gander, it's time to be fed," retorts her hungry brother. "For weeks I have eaten only bread. Life's not worth living—I wish I were dead!"

While Gretel searches the empty cupboards for crumbs, Hansel climbs down from the hayloft, still grumbling about his hunger pains.

"If you'll stop complaining, I'll tell you a secret," she offers. "Look, I found a jug of milk. I hope Mother makes a pudding tonight."

Hansel, who cannot resist the creamy milk, sticks his hand into the pitcher and greedily licks his fingers. Gretel is shocked when he then lifts the pitcher to his mouth.

"Stop!" she shouts, wresting the jug from his hands. "If we don't finish our work, there'll be trouble when Mother comes home."

Reluctantly, Hansel returns to his broommaking.

"But Gretel, work is so dull. I'd much rather be singing and dancing."

Her eyes twinkling, Gretel dances to a merry tune.

"Hansel, come and dance with me! It's as easy as can be."

Hansel begs Gretel to teach him how to dance, and he eagerly follows her instructions. Brother and sister have a wonderful time, growing wilder and happier with each spin about the room.

Now, unseen by Hansel and Gretel, their mother has neared the cottage, and, through the window, catches a glimpse of the children tossing broom twigs in the air as they sing and dance.

"So! I've caught you both misbehaving."

The happy tune comes to an abrupt end. Ashamed of herself, Gretel tries to blame Hansel, while Hansel, who feels just as guilty, accuses Gretel.

"Enough! Have you finished your chores? Let me see what you've done."

Gertrude discovers the abandoned knitting, and, as punishment, sends her daughter to bed without supper. When Hansel sticks out his tongue, his mother tries to spank him, but he runs away from her. Chasing the boy around the kitchen table, she grabs at him, misses, and knocks over the pitcher.

"Now what will we eat?" she cries, staring helplessly at the puddle of milk on the floor.

When Gretel giggles, her mother furiously orders her to come down from the loft. Gertrude thrusts a straw basket at Hansel and in a high, raging voice, issues an angry command: "Go to the woods and pick wild strawberries. If the basket isn't full when you come home, I'll whip you both!"

And Gretel follows Hansel out of the door to gather fruit for their supper.

Gertrude wipes up the milk and prays for help to feed her starving children. Then, exhausted, she sits at the kitchen table and falls asleep, bathed in the amber light of the sun's last rays.

Soon Peter's deep voice is heard in the distance, singing a haunting melody: "Tra-la-la-la, tra-la-la-la, hunger is a wicked curse!" As he draws near the cottage, his song grows louder.

"Oh, the poor man's life is weary. Every day is long and dreary."

His booming voice wakes Gertrude, who scolds him for being late, drunk, and lazy. Ignoring her complaints, he pats her affectionately.

"Cheer up, Mother, I have a wonderful surprise!"

Peter hands his knapsack to his wife, who reaches into the bag and in amazement pulls out eggs, sausage, bacon, and coffee.

"Time for us to celebrate," sings Peter. "I was in town, and my brooms were in such demand that I sold them all for a great deal of money."

In the midst of toasting their success, Peter asks where the children are. Gertrude tells him of the afternoon's sorry events and how she sent them to the forest to pick berries for supper.

"To the forest? How could you? You must be insane!"

The light dims as dark clouds cross the setting sun.

"Heavens! What do you mean?" Gertrude asks, lighting a candle.

Peter's body casts a huge black shadow on the cottage wall.

"The forest there is enchanted, and in the deepest reaches the evil ones dwell," he explains.

Peter fetches a broom and straddles it like a horse, his shadow bouncing on the walls and ceiling. An ominous melody accompanies him as he tells of the hobbling, gobbling witches who, at midnight, fly over hill and dale, in league with the powers of hell.

"And there is one witch," sings Peter, "who eats all day, in a scrunching, crunching, munching way. She lures the children into her den with tempting treats of gingerbread men. Then each poor little tot, in an oven made hot, with fire bright red, is baked into bread!"

Horrified by his tale, Gertrude rushes from the house to look for her helpless children. Peter follows to help save Hansel and Gretel from a bitter fate.

Act II

Deep in the forest, Hansel picks strawberries while Gretel weaves a wreath of wild roses and dreamily gazes at the sun setting behind the fir trees.

"Look, Gretel, my basket is full to the brim. Let's hurry home so Mother doesn't worry."

But Gretel, ignoring her brother's advice, places the wreath on his head. Hansel removes the garland and with it crowns Gretel queen of the wood. Bowing like a dutiful subject, he offers her a gift of strawberries. While Hansel and Gretel sample the fruit, a cuckoo calls and the children imitate its voice. Distracted by the bird, they absentmindedly eat the berries, and, before they know it, the basket is empty.

"Quick, we had better pick some more," cries Gretel.

But the sun has set and the night is rapidly closing in around them.

"We'll find no berries now," worries Hansel. "I doubt that we'll even find our way home."

The children search in vain for a path, as the forest comes alive with scratchings and rustles and groans. The trees sprout horrid faces, their branches waving like arms, and eyes gleam through the leaves, staring unblinkingly at the frightened children.

"Who's there?" asks Hansel bravely, trying to protect his sister.

A strange echo answers him, frightening Gretel even more.

Meanwhile, great and small creatures have been creeping out from their forest homes. Slowly and silently, owls, frogs, squirrels, dragonflies, trolls, bats, and bears surround the unsuspecting children. Then suddenly, in the distance, a lantern glows, lighting a stranger's face. The music becomes agitated as the animals run for shelter, and the children huddle together for protection. But instead of the ogre they anticipate, a kindly old man in a stocking cap approaches, singing a gentle lullaby. Reaching deep into his sack, the Sandman tosses glittering grains of sand over Hansel, Gretel, squirrel, deer, turtle, rabbit, and fox alike. The children yawn and, to a heavenly melody, say their bedtime prayers: "When at night I go to sleep, fourteen angels watch do keep. Watch above me, Lord, I pray, through the night 'till break of day."

Gretel lies down on the moss, and Hansel removes his threadbare jacket and tenderly covers her. Then, side by side, they fall fast asleep.

A dim light appears in the sky. As it glows stronger and brighter, a golden staircase is revealed, winding its way to heaven. To the music of distant bells, fourteen angels glide down the steps. After covering Hansel and Gretel with a silken blanket, the angels hover over the sleeping children, guarding their little charges through the night.

Act III

As dawn breaks in the forest, a high, clear voice rings out: "Wake up! Wake up!" The Dew Fairy, dressed in a shimmering robe, scatters dewdrops from a bluebell on the sleeping children.

Yawning and stretching, Gretel rises. She tickles and prods Hansel, and, when he wakes, she tells him of her fantastic dream.

"A host of angels, softly singing, floated down from heaven right over there!" Gretel points to a grove of pine trees.

"How strange! I had the same dream."

But when the children turn toward the trees, instead of angels, they see a great candy house rising like magic out of the morning fog. Lathered in swirls of pink frosting, the cottage, with a peppermint chimney and shutters of chocolate chips, tempts them to enter through a neat little hedge of gingerbread men.

"Can't you see how that house is smiling at us? The angels must have guided us here," says Hansel.

Gretel needs little convincing. The children tiptoe toward the house, steal a giant chocolate chip from the shutter, and sneak away to devour their prize.

A faraway voice sings out, "Nibble, nibble mousekin, who's nibbling at my housekin?"

"The wind, it must be the wind," the children decide.

Running back to the cottage, they pull a large chunk of cake from the front door,

exposing a mysterious face, aglow in an eerie green light. But Hansel and Gretel fail to notice that they are being stared at hungrily by an old witch.

"Gobble, gobble mousekin, who's gobbling up my housekin?"

The children shrug their shoulders and ignore the second warning, stuffing more and more candy into their mouths.

Silently, the witch emerges from the house and sneaks toward the unsuspecting children. Cackling loudly, she pounces and, grabbing each child tightly by the wrist, sweetly sings: "So nice of you to visit. My name's Rosina Daintymouth. I love children—especially to eat!"

"Let go of me!" shrieks Hansel.

The witch obliges, but with a beckoning finger and sly smile she tempts the children. "I have lovely peppermint chocolate drops, Turkish delight, and lollipops."

The more candy she offers, the more suspicious they become.

"Why don't you come inside, Gretel," the old hag coaxes.

"But what will you do with Hansel?"

"He's too skinny. I think I'll stuff him full of pastry to make him fat and tasty."

Hansel realizes now that Rosina Daintymouth is a witch and means them harm, and he yells to Gretel to run. But as they dash this way and that to escape, enchanted forest creatures, under the witch's command, surround them. The sky blackens, thunder rolls, and a magic wand materializes in the witch's hand. A hush comes over the forest as she points the wand at the fleeing children and chants, "Hocus, pocus, bonus, jocus," immobilizing her victims. Then, leaving Gretel frozen in place, she shoves Hansel into a wooden cage.

When the wicked witch disappears into the house for more sweets to fatten up Hansel, he warns Gretel: "Do everything she says, but watch carefully. We must learn how she works her spells."

Laughing demoniacally, the witch returns. "Come, you must eat till you die," she croons and places a cake beside Hansel's cage. Then, turning to his sister, she waves her wand and recites: "Hocus pocus elderbush! Magic spell is broken, whoosh! Now go inside, my pet, and set the table for a feast."

Gretel hurries into the house, but, instead of working, she stands at the window and eavesdrops.

When the witch checks the cage to see if her prisoner has eaten his cake, she finds him snoring loudly. But Hansel is only pretending to sleep.

"Oh, let him have his last nap. I'll dine on luscious Gretel first."

Clouds of smoke rise from the witch's huge outdoor oven. The old hag opens the iron door and fans the flames with her skirts; then, rubbing her hands together with glee, she bursts into song.

"When Gretel peeks in the oven, it's then I'll give her a shove in! One little push, wham! Make the door slam! After she's cooked and done, won't that be fun!"

To celebrate, Rosina calls her broom, and it flies to her across the forest clearing. The delirious witch hops onto her broomstick and rides into the sky. Gretel runs out of the house to watch her mad flight.

All the insects and animals, buzzing and growling, converge in the yard. Together they tremble as the cackling crone rides high and low over their heads, to the accompaniment of crashing cymbals and pounding drums.

"Whoa, broomstick, whoa!" The witch quickly descends from the sky, landing near Hansel's cage. "Stick out your thumb, skinny."

Instead, clever Hansel holds out a chicken bone.

"You're as lean as a skeleton. Quick, Gretel, bring me raisins to fatten him up."

While Rosina feeds Hansel raisins, Gretel cautiously tiptoes to the oven and steals the magic wand from the ledge where the witch has left it.

"Hocus pocus elderbush, magic spell is broken, whoosh!" she chants.

The witch is too busy to notice Gretel's trickery. When the crone leaves Hansel's side to check the oven again, Gretel hides the wand and unlocks her brother's cage.

"Gretel, my sweet," Rosina cajoles, "look in the oven and see if my cookies are done."

Hansel whispers a warning to Gretel as she walks toward the oven. She stretches to open the door, but pretends she can't reach it.

"It's no use," she complains. "It's much too high."

"It's simple," scoffs the witch. "Stand up on tiptoe, tilt your head just so."

"I'm such a goose. I don't understand. Show me how."

Impatiently muttering, "Here's how it's done," the witch opens the door, bends forward, and leans into the oven. Hansel escapes from the cage, and brother and sister together shove the old hag into the oven. Bang! They slam the door shut. The fire crackles and smoke billows from the chimney.

"The witch is really dead! We have no more to dread!" they sing joyfully.

All the animals, released from the witch's spell, come out of hiding to greet their saviors. Then, with sudden force, the oven explodes, triggering a miraculous event: the hedge of gingerbread men falls away to reveal dozens of children, who had been baked into gingerbread by the witch. They stand motionless, their eyes sealed shut, still under the witch's spell.

Hansel and Gretel wander among the children, who unite in song: "We are safe! We are free! Our thanks to you!"

To erase the witch's spell and restore their lost sight, Gretel touches the face of each and every child. To release their frozen bodies, Hansel waves the witch's wand, reciting her magic chant.

As everyone gives thanks to the angels for wisely guiding Hansel and Gretel to the witch's lair, a familiar voice is heard in the distance singing, "Tra-la-la-la, tra-la-la-la. I can't believe they'd come this far."

"Father! Mother!" cry Hansel and Gretel, and, as the family is reunited, four boys pull a gingerbread witch from the ruins of the oven. It is the wicked Rosina Daintymouth, baked to perfection.

All the children join Peter in a song of thanks. Then, dancing and twirling in dizzy circles, everyone rejoices in their good fortune.

The curtain falls

Prologue

On either side of a gaily decorated stage, the balconies are overflowing with noisy spectators. From the wings, a group of Tragedians walk onto the proscenium.

"Give us tragedies!" they demand in deep, solemn voices, brandishing their umbrellas.

From the opposite side of the stage, the Comedians retort: "No, give us comedies!"

"A love story!" chime in the Romanticists from the left balcony.

"Slapstick!" cry the Empty Heads from the right.

In a fury, the Romanticists and the Empty Heads climb onto the stage to do battle. Ten Eccentrics, armed with gigantic shovels, file out from behind the curtain and force everyone back to their seats.

"You will see incomparable theater, a true spectacle—*The Love for Three Oranges*!" they sing as the curtain rises.

A single bass trombone announces the herald.

"The King of Clubs is heartbroken," the herald tells the expectant audience, "because his only son suffers from incurable hypochondria."

Melancholy music accompanies his introduction, but soon livelier chords are struck and the action unfolds.

Act I

In a stuffy, overheated room, the royal physicians surround the prince, poking and prodding his skinny body with their medical instruments. The King of Clubs, with a heavy heart, asks what is wrong with his poor son.

Singing in harmony, the physicians offer their diagnosis.

"He has liver trouble, asthma, backache, chronic cough, bad eyes, anemia, heartburn, dizziness, fainting fits, insomnia, dark presentiments, total apathy, and profound melancholy. In short . . . hypochondria."

"Your prognosis?"

"Incurable!" reply the doctors, withdrawing from the room with their patient.

"I'm old," moans the king with tears in his eyes. "Who will succeed me?"

The king's chief fear is that his cruel and unscrupulous niece, Clarissa, may inherit the throne if his son dies.

"Now the doctors say my son's condition is hopeless, but once they recommended laughter as a cure," recalls the king.

"Then let's make him laugh," urges Pantaloon, the king's loyal adviser.

At first the king is doubtful, but after some gentle persuasion Pantaloon prevails, and Truffaldino, the court jester, is summoned.

To a lighthearted tune, Truffaldino somersaults into the room.

"What can I do for you?" asks the clown, leaping into the air, catching hold of a crystal chandelier, and swinging precariously on it.

"I would like you to make my son laugh."

"I will arrange for the festivities at once," sings Truffaldino cheerfully as he jumps off his high perch and tumbles out through the door.

The king then summons Leandro, his prime minister. With a solemn air, the black-robed Leandro enters, and the king charges him to organize merry games. From their balcony, the Eccentrics cheer: "Festivals, games, masquerades!"

"It will only tire the prince," Leandro protests.

"Nevertheless, we must try," pronounces the king.

"Traitor," curses Pantaloon, convinced that Leandro wishes the prince's death.

"Buffoon!" retorts Leandro, before the stage grows dark and the curtain falls.

*   *   *

But this is no ordinary stage curtain: it glows with an intense cadmium-red light, the color of the inferno. To ominous strains, Celio the magician climbs out from his lair through an open trap door. Lightning streaks and thunder roars as the fiendish witch, Fata Morgana, emerges from the bowels of hell and confronts the wizard. Morgana and Celio are arch enemies, locked in a deadly duel for the King of Clubs' throne. Fata Morgana, Leandro's protector, is bent on destroying the prince and installing her protégé as ruler. Celio, guardian spirit of the king, wages war with the witch in a card game with the crown at stake. Little red devils, lugging a table and a deck of playing cards, surface through the open trap door. They place the table between the adversaries, and Celio deals the first hand.

Cards are chosen and discarded, one after another. Like a swarm of bees, the little devils buzz and dance in circles around the players.

"Poor king! Leandro is winning," cry the Eccentrics.

"Ha-ha-ha!" cackles Fata Morgana, victoriously raising the trump card.

Her game won, the sorceress disappears. The others leave the stage as the light of the underworld dissolves and the curtain rises.

*   *   *

Inside the palace, Leandro and Clarissa plot against the king. Horns and strings accompany their scheming voices.

"Remember, if the prince dies, I will inherit the throne and marry you," sings Clarissa, allowing Leandro to kiss her hand. "But to be worthy of my hand, you must be daring."

"Patience," responds Leandro, his deep baritone rising with glee. "I feed him tragic verse with his bread and soup. He'll soon die of hypochondriac nightmares."

Exasperated by this ineffectual method, Clarissa draws a gun and waves it at Leandro. "Poison or a bullet," she demands.

Playful music distracts them from their devilish schemes. Truffaldino and his helpers parade by, hauling props and devices for the great festival.

"Who is that?" Clarissa asks Leandro in amazement.

He explains that Truffaldino has been employed by the king to cure the prince with laughter.

"Do you see what your indecision has led to? Give him poison or a bullet before his health is restored."

A loud noise startles them. A vase has fallen to the floor and lies in pieces. Leandro discovers the red-haired servant girl, Smeraldina, hiding under the table.

"Execute her for spying!" shouts the minister.

"Wait! I can help you," the girl cries, revealing that she is Fata Morgana's handmaiden. "Laughter can still be avoided tomorrow, because Fata Morgana is on your side. Whenever the witch is near him, the prince will not laugh."

The schemers are awestruck.

"Fata Morgana," they sing fervently, "come to the festival!"

Act II

The pale, sickly prince languishes in his armchair. Beside him is a silver tray filled with medicine bottles.

Truffaldino stands on his head and wiggles his toes. "Is that funny?"

"How can anything be funny when my eyes burn and my stomach aches?"

Truffaldino suspects that bad rhymes are the cause of the prince's discomfort, and the Eccentrics, jeering from their balcony, accuse Leandro of poisoning his sick highness with rotten verse.

"Come to the festival," Truffaldino invites the prince. "There's fun and amusement in store."

At the mention of these tantalizing words, the Comedians bound onto the proscenium, hailing the jester's plan. The Eccentrics, armed with shovels, chase the intruders from the stage. As they all return to the balconies, the strains of a joyful march are heard.

"Let's hurry," sings Truffaldino excitedly, and he hurls the medicine tray out of the window.

Too weak to resist, the horrified prince is wrapped in a cloak, lifted onto Truffaldino's shoulders, and carried off.

*   *   *

On a terrace overlooking the palace courtyard, the king and his entire court are seated. For the first entertainment, two hairy monsters, their heads the size of watermelons, battle with clubs.

"Bravo!" applauds the crowd.

"All this noise makes my head ache," whines the prince.

While Truffaldino prepares the next amusement, Fata Morgana, disguised as an old woman, slouches into the courtyard. Leandro takes her aside and demands to know who she is.

"I am Fata Morgana. The prince will not laugh while I'm here."

Dropping to his knees, Leandro sings in gratitude, "Benefactress, O Queen of Hypochondria!"

"Entertainment number two," announces Truffaldino.

Two fountains—one of oil, one of wine—begin gushing. An army of drunkards and gluttons charges into the courtyard, trying to fill their pails and cups.

"Bravo!" cheers the crowd.

"Tuck me into my cozy bed," pleads the prince.

Truffaldino despairs of ever curing the prince and dismisses the actors. He tries to shoo away Fata Morgana, but the witch refuses to leave. Her willfulness enrages Truffaldino, who chases her around the courtyard and gives the old hag a push. Her feet fly out from under her and she lands helplessly on her back.

A strange sound escapes the prince's throat. Is it possible? Could this be a laugh?

"That old woman is funny!" he giggles.

The guests cheer, the king dances on his throne, Truffaldino turns somersaults. Only Clarissa and Leandro are unmoved.

But as Fata Morgana rises to her feet, dark clouds obscure the sun.

"Barbarian, listen to my curse!" she howls, and commands the prince to fall madly in love with three oranges.

"Day and night, run, run. Search the ends of the earth for the three oranges."

The sorceress disappears in a puff of blue smoke. The prince, in desperate haste to find the oranges, calls for his sword and armor.

The king knows the three oranges are guarded by Creonta, a murderous witch, and is certain his son faces a gruesome death. But, try as he may, he is powerless to change the prince's mind.

Farfarello, a cloven-hoofed devil, hops onto the terrace carrying an enormous bellows. He sets a whirlwind in motion, blowing the prince and a protesting Truffaldino into the sky and away.

Act III

Under a starry sky, the magician, Celio, wanders through the desert calling, "Farfarello! Farfarello!"

Poking his head out of the sand, the devil asks, "Who calls me from the depths of darkness?"

Celio wishes to know the whereabouts of the prince and the jester. Farfarello explains that he is blowing them to Creonta's castle. Knowing that such a visit could spell their doom, Celio orders the devil to stop his cruel pranks.

"A magician who loses at cards has no power over me," Farfarello laughs and disappears.

The prince and Truffaldino slide down a sand dune, landing beside Celio. The magician urges them to give up their search.

"A dreadful cook guards the three oranges day and night. She will attack you with her deadly soup ladle."

The prince refuses to heed Celio's warning. Truffaldino, however, is terrified and collapses on the sand. To give him courage, Celio hands the jester a magic ribbon to wave before the cook's eyes. If the spell works, the ribbon will distract her long enough to allow the prince to steal the oranges.

"But remember, if you obtain the three oranges, they must be opened near water. If they are not, disaster will befall you."

Farfarello reappears with his bellows and blows them into the sky with the power of a cannon blast.

"Beware the ladle," sings Celio as they disappear into the heavens.

*   *   *

Lively violins accompany their dizzying flight. Then suddenly, without warning, the swirling rhythms of horns and drums announce an abrupt landing at Creonta's castle.

The prince, bent on stealing the oranges, takes the quaking Truffaldino by the collar and drags him into the kitchen. There, astride an enormous oven, its flames darting red, stands a gigantic cook.

"Who's there, whining and sniveling?" she howls. "I'll flatten you with my ladle and toss you in the dustbin."

"Please, noble lady. There's been a mistake," Truffaldino croons piteously, cowering behind Celio's magic ribbon.

"What's that?" asks the cook. "It's charming . . . I feel quite lightheaded when I gaze upon it."

Suddenly subdued and almost friendly, the cook asks Truffaldino to give her the ribbon. As Truffaldino edges closer to the cook, dangling the ribbon under her nose, the prince runs from the kitchen clutching three perfect oranges, the size of human heads.

"Here you are. Something to remember me by," sings Truffaldino saucily, tossing her the ribbon and darting out of the kitchen door.

*   *   *

As the prince and his jester cross the vast desert, a strange transformation takes place: the three oranges slowly become so large that they can no longer be carried. They must now be rolled with enormous effort across the shifting sands.

Eventually, the weary prince lies down and falls asleep. Truffaldino, however, is too thirsty to rest. Eyeing a fragrant orange, he picks up his sword.

"Juicy orange," the jester sings rhapsodically, "I had better eat you and save my life."

With a swift chop, he cuts the fruit open. To his amazement, a lovely maiden, dressed all in white, emerges from the hollow fruit.

"I am Princess Linetta," she begins sweetly, but then stops short, clutching her throat. "A drink, or I will die of thirst!"

"I had better open another orange to quench the poor girl's thirst."

With a slash of his blade, Truffaldino opens a second orange. Once again, a lovely maiden, dressed in white, emerges.

"I am Princess Nicoletta," she sings sweetly. But in the next moment, she, too, gasps for breath.

Princess Linetta cries out, "Take pity!" But before she can utter another word, she dies. Next, Princess Nicoletta falls to the ground. Raising a hand toward the jester, she begs for mercy; then she too dies.

The terrified clown runs away. When the royal heir awakes, he finds two dead princesses lying at his feet.

As he ponders their mysterious deaths, four soldiers march onto the scene. Accustomed to giving orders, the prince commands the soldiers to bury the maidens, and they carry the bodies away.

But the prince's curiosity has been aroused, and he opens the third orange. Yet another maiden rises from the hollow fruit, but this one is far more beautiful than the others.

"I am Princess Ninetta," she sings sweetly.

"Princess, I have been searching the four corners of the earth for you."

But his happiness is short-lived, for in the next moment the princess clutches her throat and gasps for breath. "Quickly, a drink or I shall die of thirst!"

The Eccentrics, annoyed by all this death, carry a bucket of water onto the stage. Ninetta drinks and revives.

"Thank you, prince," she sings in a high, clear voice. "You have saved me from death and released me from bondage. I love you."

The prince invites Ninetta to the palace to meet his father, but she refuses.

"Speak to your father first, then bring me regal robes so that I may be presented to him in the proper fashion."

The prince agrees and they part happily.

As night falls, Smeraldina, wielding an enormous hat pin, sneaks up behind the princess. With a swift thrust of the pin, Smeraldina pierces Ninetta's forehead, transforming her into a huge rat. Ninetta scurries away, and Smeraldina, dressed in a white gown and veil, takes the princess's place on the sand.

Soon a cheerful march can be heard, heralding the arrival of the court. The happy prince introduces his father to his bride-to-be; but when the prince lifts her veil, he discovers a strange red-haired woman.

"This isn't my princess!"

"I am Princess Ninetta and you promised to marry me," whines Smeraldina.

The king declares that a royal promise is a promise that must be kept. Unwillingly, the prince offers Smeraldina his hand, and the procession departs for court.

Act IV

In front of the glowing red curtain, in the sizzling underworld, Celio and Fata Morgana confront each other.

"Fallen witch, resorting to hat pins!" mocks Celio.

"Children's party magician, playing with ribbons!" scorns Fata Morgana in a high-pitched squeal.

Sick to death of Fata Morgana's meddling, the Eccentrics climb down from their balcony and lock the witch in a room next to the stage.

A boastful Celio, taking credit for silencing the witch, leaves to save the royal family from Leandro and his accomplices.

*   *   *

To strains of the gay little march, the royal procession enters the throne room. Leandro signals for the drapery before the thrones to be parted and there, sitting on the princess's throne, is Ninetta the rat. Everyone, on stage and off, shrieks. In the midst of the turmoil, Celio appears and, waving his arms, transforms the rat back into the real princess.

"Yes, this is my princess, my love, my orange," cries the prince with joy.

"Then who is this other woman?" the king asks, pointing to the fake princess.

Bounding in from nowhere, Truffaldino answers, "Smeraldina!"

Deducing that Smeraldina is the secret accomplice of Leandro and the wicked Clarissa, the king pronounces sentence.

"Let the three of them be hanged for treason. Guards, bring the rope."

Smeraldina, in terror, runs for her life. Clarissa and Leandro race behind her, panting and screaming. The guards dash off in pursuit, followed by Pantaloon, Truffaldino, and the courtiers.

Meanwhile, Fata Morgana has managed to break down her prison door. She extends her arms to the three traitors and, safe in her embrace, the fiends disappear into hell as dark clouds shroud their descent and drums pound menacingly.

After all this terrible confusion, the world grows quiet and the sky clears.

"Long live the king!" shout the Eccentrics.

"Long live the prince and princess!" amends the king.

"Long live our king, prince and princess!" everyone sings joyously.

The curtain falls

Act I

Pursued by a giant serpent, Prince Tamino flees across a rocky landscape. "Merciful gods, protect me!" he cries.

As the jaws of the monster are about to close on the prince, three veiled women appear and kill the beast with their silver javelins. Tamino lies motionless on the ground beside the slain serpent.

"We saved this youth from certain death," sing the proud heroines, as they admire the handsome boy. The three women, ladies-in-waiting to a queen, bid a reluctant farewell to the youth and go to tell their sovereign about him.

"Where am I?" asks Tamino, awakening from his faint. He slowly rises to his feet, wondering how he so miraculously escaped the jaws of death.

Tamino's attention is diverted by what sounds like the call of a bird. He sees a strange figure, dressed in a multicolored suit of feathers, coming down a path, an enormous birdcage strapped to his back. Tamino hides behind a tree as the creature plays his panpipes and bursts into a merry song.

"My trade is catching birds, you know; I spread my nets and in they go. And all men know me as a friend throughout the land, from end to end."

The fellow lures the birds with his pipes and fills his cage, but he wishes he could snare dozens of young maidens instead.

"I'd choose the one who loved me best and make her my wife," he sings jubilantly.

Tamino, coming out from behind the tree, extends a hand and introduces himself as a prince, son of a mighty king who rules over many countries.

"And who are you?"

"Papageno," answers the birdcatcher. "I live alone in a snug little hut and catch birds for the queen. Her ladies pay me in food and drink."

Suspecting that this queen is none other than the powerful Queen of the Night, Tamino questions Papageno further, but the birdcatcher grows suspicious.

"Keep your distance!"

Clenching his fists and flexing his muscles, he boasts, "I'll have you know I've got the strength of a giant."

"Then it must be you who slew the serpent," says Tamino gratefully, pointing to the dead monster.

The birdcatcher quivers with fear at the sight of the beast, but, wishing to appear strong and powerful, he accepts Tamino's thanks.

"Papageno!" a trio of familiar voices call warningly.

The Three Ladies suddenly reappear, and instead of the usual reward for his birdcatching, Papageno is punished for lying. The women attach a golden padlock to his mouth, and he is unable to utter a word.

Before they leave, the Three Ladies present the prince with a locket containing a small portrait.

"Our sovereign sends you this picture of her daughter, Pamina. If she pleases you, happiness, honor, and glory await you."

Spellbound by Pamina's beauty, Tamino gazes intently at the portrait and sings a love song to this unknown princess.

As he kisses her portrait, the Three Ladies return.

"Noble youth, our queen has heard your song and said: 'If his courage is as strong as his love, I will show him the way to rescue Pamina from Sarastro, the evil magician who has stolen her away.'"

Thundering drums and majestic violins announce the arrival of the Queen of the Night. The sky grows dark and stars blaze in the heavens, as the mountains part to reveal the Queen seated on her throne of stars.

In a magnificent soprano, she laments the loss of her child, promising Tamino Pamina's hand in marriage if he rescues her from Sarastro's domain. Powerless to save her daughter, her voice trembles with emotion at the prospect of defeating her enemy and regaining her child. In a fit of grief and rage, she disappears.

"Was I dreaming?" Tamino wonders, as the sky lightens.

Poor Papageno's muffled cries reach the prince's ears, drawing him back to reality.

"Hm, hm, hm!" groans the birdcatcher, pointing to the padlock.

Try as he may, Tamino is unable to release Papageno from the golden lock. Luckily, the Three Ladies return with word that the Queen has taken pity on Papageno. On condition that he never lie again, he will be freed. The birdcatcher readily promises to be truthful.

A gift from the Queen is bestowed on Tamino—a magic flute to guard him against danger. To induce a reluctant Papageno to accompany the prince to Sarastro's secret temple, the Three Ladies give him a silver glockenspiel to enchant his enemies. Papageno consents, and the five sing their farewells.

"But which way is the temple?" asks the prince.

To a tender, pure melody, the Three Ladies sing: "Three Genii will guide you. These young boys are fair, gentle, and wise."

"We will do as they say. Farewell," sing the departing heroes.

In a sumptuous room in Sarastro's palace, three slaves anxiously discuss Pamina's escape from her evil keeper, the Moor Monostatos. At that moment, the voice of their master rings out: "Slaves! Bring me chains and fetters!" And Monostatos drags Pamina back into the room.

Poor Pamina begs the heartless Moor to spare her and faints. Commanding the slaves to leave him alone with Pamina, Monostatos is about to kiss her, when Papageno pokes his head through the open window. The birdcatcher recognizes the sleeping girl, climbs through the window, and slowly approaches. Monostatos thinks the intruder is a demonic bird and Papageno imagines the Moor to be the devil. Both shriek, "It's Lucifer himself!" then turn and run in opposite directions.

But Papageno is determined to conquer his fear and save the princess. He returns to the room and greets the girl as the daughter of the Queen of the Night.

"You know me? Are you a messenger from my mother?"

Papageno shows Pamina the portrait in the locket, explaining how he came to have it and describing the handsome prince who has fallen in love with her. Pamina is very pleased to be loved by a noble youth and asks where he is.

"Tamino sent me ahead to find you while he searches for the Three Genii who are to guide us through Sarastro's realm."

A grateful Pamina praises Papageno for his good heart.

"What good does it do me when Papageno has no Papagena to love."

"Heaven will send you a wife," Pamina assures him, and together they sing tenderly of the joys of love and devotion. Then, holding hands, they flee Sarastro's castle.

*   *   *

Meanwhile, in a grove near three temples, the Genii counsel Tamino to be steadfast, patient, and silent. Tamino, determined to follow their advice, approaches the temples.

"This seems a place where gods dwell. I'll walk through each door. My purpose is worthy and honest. Tremble, cruel sorcerer! I vow to save Pamina."

As the prince tries to enter the first temple, a commanding voice from within calls: "Go back!" Tamino obeys and approaches the second door. Again, a voice proclaims: "Go back!"

The prince knocks on the door of the last temple. It swings open and there, bathed in light, stands an elderly priest.

"What brings you to this temple, bold stranger?" asks the priest.

"I seek love and truth."

"Love and truth have not led you here. Only death and vengeance."

"Vengeance, yes, for the villain Sarastro."

"You have been deceived," declares the priest in a serene voice. "There are no villains here. In time, Sarastro will reveal his true purpose in taking Pamina away from her mother."

Tamino drops to his knees in despair.

"When will this veil of darkness be lifted?" he beseeches.

"When you join our holy order in friendship," answers the old priest, disappearing into the temple.

Left alone to ponder these mysteries, Tamino sings out, "When will light dispel my blindness?"

An unseen chorus softly answers him: "Soon . . . or never."

Confused and uncertain, Tamino begs to know if Pamina is still alive. When the voices answer yes, Tamino rejoices, playing the magic flute in celebration. His charming, pastoral melody is so beautiful that it draws the wild beasts from the forest. Lions, bears, giraffes, and monkeys listen in an enchanted trance.

Wondering why Pamina doesn't appear too, Tamino plays five quick notes on his flute. To his delight, Papageno answers, playing his familiar birdcall on the panpipes. The prince runs off in the direction of Papageno's pipes, followed by a line of dancing beasts.

*　　*　　*

Hand in hand, Pamina and Papageno search the palace grounds for Tamino. Unfortunately, before they can find him, Monostatos discovers them in the sacred grove.

"I shall clap you both in irons, then I'll feed you to the lions," he sings triumphantly.

Before he can be chained by the Moor's slaves, the resourceful Papageno plays a little tune on his magic glockenspiel. The enchanted Moor and his slaves dance on tiptoe down a path and out of sight.

Praising the magic bells in song, the princess and the birdcatcher wish all honest men could have a set of these wondrous bells to ward off trouble and discord. At the conclusion of their duet, a fanfare of trumpets and drums heralds Sarastro's return from the hunt.

"We are lost," cries Pamina.

"Lord deliver us from evil!" quakes Papageno.

A procession of loyal disciples, singing their leader's praises in a mighty chorus, precedes Sarastro. The monarch wears a golden medallion around his neck—the sevenfold circle of the sun. He stops before Pamina and Papageno.

"Forgive me," the princess begs. "I did attempt to escape, but the blame is not all mine. I was fleeing the wicked Moor."

"Be at peace," proclaims Sarastro in a deep, powerful voice. "I know your heart's secret." Divining that she loves a young man, he understands her wish to join her suitor. "I don't want to deny your love, yet it is too soon to grant your freedom."

Pamina now claims that her duty as a daughter impels her to return to her mother.

"Your future happiness would be lost forever if I allowed you to rejoin that woman. My wisdom shall guide you."

Monostatos enters, dragging Tamino behind him. Pamina calls his name, and the prince, seeing his true love at last, embraces her. Monostatos begs Sarastro to punish the foreigners for attempting to kidnap Pamina.

"It is you who have earned a just reward for your spying," declares Sarastro. "Seventy-seven lashes!"

"That's not the reward I had hoped for!" shrieks the struggling Moor as he is dragged away.

Welcoming the two strangers to his land, Sarastro bids his priests to blindfold them and bring them to the temple to be purified. Noble music celebrates the high purpose of this brotherhood of men, as Tamino and Papageno are led away.

Act II

To a solemn march, eighteen high priests gather in a palm grove behind the temple. Sarastro declares that it is their duty to watch over Tamino and help him to find enlightenment. All deem him worthy to brave the difficult tests of the Initiates.

Sarastro then explains that the gods have singled out the virtuous Pamina to be Tamino's bride.

"For this reason I took Pamina away from her mother. If the princess is to defend our temple at Tamino's side, she must be free of her arrogant mother who wishes to destroy our order through deceit and superstition."

Sarastro sends two priests to lead the prince and his companion into the courtyard for instruction. And, in a hymn of beautiful simplicity, Sarastro asks the gods to protect Tamino and Papageno.

*   *   *

Night has fallen when Tamino and Papageno are left in the courtyard.

"What a fearful night! Papageno, are you still there?"

"Yes . . . more's the pity."

The priests emerge from the temple. "Stranger, what brings you to our sanctuary?"

"Friendship and love," answers Tamino.

When asked if he is willing to undergo every trial, to fight for his principles with his life, Tamino fearlessly accepts. Papageno, on the other hand, wishes only for food, drink, and a pretty wife. But when he is told that Sarastro has chosen a Papagena for him, he agrees to follow Tamino.

Both Tamino and Papageno are sworn to silence as their first trial. Cautioning them to be on their guard against the wiles of women, the priests depart.

Just as Tamino begs a softly chattering Papageno to keep silent, the Three Ladies appear. In their exquisite, airy voices, they threaten the prince and his companion with destruction if they continue to heed the words of the priests.

Tamino counsels Papageno to be quiet, and assures him that they speak nonsense. The women beg to know why they are treated so coldly and complain bitterly. Displeased by their wagging tongues, the priests frighten the Three Ladies away.

At last, the first trial ends and the priests return. Tamino and Papageno are congratulated on withstanding the badgering of the Queen's handmaidens before they are once again blindfolded and led away.

*   *   *

Beneath a fragrant rose arbor, in a secluded garden, Pamina lies asleep. Monostatos peers through the branches, then slowly advances toward the unsuspecting princess.

"One kiss won't do any harm," he sings, drawing nearer.

At that moment, the Queen of the Night appears in all her unearthly splendor, and drives Monostatos from the arbor. Pamina awakes to discover her mother and cries out with happiness. But it is short-lived.

"Tamino has betrayed us," says the Queen. "I can protect you no longer. My power vanished when your father died."

The Queen reveals that, on his deathbed, Pamina's father gave the all-powerful, sevenfold circle of the sun to Sarastro and his followers.

"Your father wished Sarastro to take his place as your male guardian and for us to bow to his authority, but I cannot obey a tyrant who wishes my destruction."

The Queen orders her daughter to persuade Tamino to renounce Sarastro. Bewildered by her mother's command, Pamina defends her guardian, maintaining that her father trusted in his wisdom.

Enraged, the Queen of the Night hurls a dagger to the ground.

"I command you to kill Sarastro!"

Pamina stares fearfully at the dagger, while the Queen cries for vengeance, threatening to disown her daughter if she fails to kill Sarastro. Her beautiful voice no longer comforts Pamina. It has become the messenger of evil.

When the Queen vanishes, Monostatos, who has been spying on them, confronts Pamina with the dark plot he has just overheard.

"I know of your murderous scheme. There is only one way to save yourself and your mother from Sarastro's punishment . . . love me!"

When Pamina pulls away from him in disgust, Monostatos threatens to kill her, pointing the dagger at her throat. Without warning, Sarastro sweeps into the garden and orders the trembling Moor to leave his land forever.

Pamina begs Sarastro to spare her mother, who has been driven mad by her daughter's absence.

"Revenge is unknown within these sacred walls," he sings reassuringly. "Love rescues those who have fallen."

Placing his arm protectively around Pamina's shoulders, he adds, "Those who reject these teachings are not worthy of the human race."

*　　*　　*

In preparation for their next trial, Tamino and Papageno are led into a great hall, opening onto a veranda. The priests instruct them to follow the trumpet calls and, above all, to remain silent. After the priests leave, Tamino waits quietly, but Papageno hops from one foot to the other, chattering to himself and wishing for a drink of water.

As if by magic, an old hag enters through a trap door and brings him a goblet.

"Come sit by me. Talk to me," Papageno urges. "How old are you, my angel?"

"Eighteen."

"Do you have a boyfriend?" jokes Papageno.

"Yes, he's twenty-eight."

"And what is his name?"

"Papageno," she exclaims, in a fit of laughter.

The birdcatcher jumps to his feet and cautiously asks her name.

"Papagena," she replies.

Before the amazed Papageno can question her further, thunder roars and the hag disappears. A hot-air balloon, carrying the Three Genii, floats down from the sky. The Genii restore the magic flute to Tamino and the silver bells to Papageno and set a table laden with delicacies before them.

"Be brave, Tamino, for your goal is near," they sing cheerfully, as the balloon floats away. "And you, Papageno, be silent."

The hungry birdcatcher devours the food, but Tamino prefers to play his flute. Pamina hears the music and runs to Tamino's side. The prince, who must honor his vow of silence, sadly motions her away.

"Don't you love me anymore?" she asks, but he refuses to answer.

The melody of flutes and strings accompanies her poignant song.

"Only in death will I find peace," she laments.

*   *   *

The priests convene at sunrise within the vault of a grand pyramid. Tamino enters and is congratulated by Sarastro for his courage.

"But two dangerous trials still await you if you wish to rule as an enlightened monarch with Pamina at your side."

Pamina is admitted to the sacred hall, and Sarastro instructs the young lovers to say farewell, promising they will meet again. The princess worries for Tamino's safety and for her place in his heart. Answering her anxious song, the two men advise Pamina to trust in Tamino's love, and Sarastro leads the prince away.

Meanwhile, Papageno wanders into the now deserted hall. He approaches the door through which Tamino has passed, but a voice orders, "Go back!" When the birdcatcher tries to leave the hall through the entry door, again a voice cautions, "Go back!"

"Now I can neither go forward nor back," he weeps.

THE MAGIC FLUTE   ACT II

At last, the speaker takes pity on Papageno, and a large goblet of wine rises magically out of the earth. The birdcatcher drinks the wine and, remembering his dreams, he longs for the joy of married life. In answer to his plea, the old hag returns.

"Here I am, my angel. If you promise to be true to me, I'll be your loving wife. Don't hesitate, or you'll be locked in here forever with only bread and water to live on."

"Oh well, better an old wife than no wife." Papageno shakes her hand, swearing to be true. "As long as I don't find anyone prettier."

Instantly, the old hag turns into a lovely young woman, dressed all in feathers.

"Papagena!" the birdcatcher marvels, opening his arms to embrace her.

At that moment the speaker appears and takes Papagena away—Papageno is still not worthy of her.

*　　*　　*

In a pleasant little garden, the Three Genii salute the rising sun, predicting that soon all evil will disappear and truth will reign.

"Then mankind will achieve the kingdom of heaven on earth."

Pamina enters the garden, grief-stricken because of Tamino's coldness and her mother's angry curses. The boys rush to her side to comfort her.

"Tamino would die if he saw you like this. He loves you."

At first, she doubts their words, but they assure her that the prince is braving death for her sake. Then, gaily joining hands, they all go in search of Tamino.

*　　*　　*

Two guards lead Tamino to the tall iron gates that bar the entryway to the trials by fire and water. Reading the inscription above the gates, the guards sing in their deep voices: "He who enters these portals faces great danger. He must be purified by fire, water, air, and earth, overcoming the fear of death itself. Only then will he soar to heaven."

Pamina is allowed to see Tamino again, and the guards confirm that he is released from his vow of silence. The couple embrace and decide to face the trials together.

"Love will be our guide," Pamina sings.

She counsels Tamino to play the magic flute while they pass through the burning fires and turbulent floods, and the sound of the flute accompanies them as they overcome their final trials.

When they emerge at last, the priests chorus: "Rejoice, you noble pair. The prize of virtue now is yours."

*   *   *

Wandering through the little garden, Papageno calls for his Papagena.

"My babbling has cost me my sweetheart. It serves me right."

The birdcatcher vows to hang himself from the nearest tree.

Floating down in their balloon, the Three Genii suggest to Papageno that he first try a tune on his magic bells. Delighted at this reminder, the birdcatcher plays the glockenspiel, hoping that Papagena will appear.

"Turn around, Papageno," sing the boys.

Papagena climbs out of the balloon and stands before her Papageno. With a shy stutter, they call each other's name, singing joyfully at the prospect of one day having a family of little Papagenas and Papagenos.

*   *   *

Meanwhile, the Queen of the Night, the Three Ladies, and Monostatos prepare to storm the temple of the Initiates. But as they approach the inner temple of the brotherhood, the evil army is met by the sun's burning rays. Shielding their eyes from the glare, they sink to the ground, helpless against the forces of light. Sarastro, whose wisdom has harnessed the sun's power, stands on high, and is joined by Tamino and Pamina.

Proclaiming the destruction of the sinful and the passing of night, Sarastro bestows the circle of the sun on the prince, while a triumphant chorus hails the two wise monarchs, Pamina and Tamino, who dared everything for truth.

The curtain falls

Act I

In the sixteenth century in the great city of Nuremberg, where a man's song was valued more highly than his gold, a guild of Mastersingers arose to cherish and preserve the art of singing.

On the vigil of the Feast of St. John, the townsfolk have assembled at church. Eva, daughter of the goldsmith and Mastersinger, Veit Pogner, sits in a pew beside her chaperone, Magdalene, exchanging glances with the young knight, Walther von Stolzing, who has just settled in Nuremberg. At the end of the chorale, the organ plays on as the congregation files out of the church. Walther approaches Eva.

"Stay! A word," he pleads. "Tell me, are you betrothed?"

They are distracted by the entrance of Magdalene's beau, David, an aspiring Mastersinger and apprentice to the cobbler Hans Sachs. He closes a black curtain around the nave of the church and disappears.

"Sir Knight, this is a difficult question to answer," begins Magdalene. "Though Eva is indeed betrothed, the bridegroom's name will not be known until tomorrow, when she will be given in marriage to the Mastersinger who wins the song contest."

A dignified melody, the theme of the Mastersingers, echoes in the quiet church.

Walther wonders aloud: "The bride will then choose. . . ."

"You and no other," Eva blurts out.

David now returns with a piece of chalk attached to a string, and he draws a circle on the stone floor—a ring for the Masters' auditions. He explains that today's song trials are open to apprentices.

"If no rules are broken, a pupil may become a Mastersinger."

"What must I do?" asks Walther, determined to become a Mastersinger and win Eva's hand.

"Let David teach you the rules of the trial," sings Magdalene, offering her beau a delicious meal if he helps the knight become a Master.

Walther promises to visit Eva that evening, and Magdalene leads her out of the door. As a group of apprentices enter the church, Walther sinks into a chair, brooding over his future.

"Now begin!" shouts David, to Walther's astonishment. "That's what the marker cries when you're to begin singing. Don't you know that?"

Walther shakes his head. David's impatience turns to disbelief when he realizes that

Walther cannot even claim to be called "school-friend" or "scholar"—the first steps on the path to Mastersinger.

"You have passed none of these tests and you expect to be a Mastersinger? I have learned everything I know from the finest Master in all Nuremberg, Hans Sachs, and I have yet to be named Master."

Eloquently describing the guild's rules, David sings out the name of each and every rhyme and melody.

"Only when a singer is able to unite rhyme and word with a melody of his own invention is he ready to be awarded the glorious title of 'Mastersinger.'"

Returning to his work, David helps the other apprentices prepare the church for the trial. The apprentices tease David for his pretensions to the title of Mastersinger, and the young cobbler points out Walther, who will dare to try his hand that day.

At the entrance of Master Veit Pogner and the pedantic old town clerk, Sixtus Beckmesser, the young men scurry to their seats. Walther greets Master Pogner and announces that he wishes to become a member of the Mastersingers' Guild. Delighted at the prospect of this good-hearted youth joining the guild and competing for his daughter's hand, Pogner agrees to propose him for membership.

As Walther prepares for his trial, the Mastersingers assemble. Hans Sachs, the cobbler, is the last to arrive—a genial old widower with a youthful bearing. Fritz Kothner, the president of the guild, steps onto the podium and calls out the names of the Masters. Each responds in turn, proudly taking his seat. Pogner asks leave to speak.

"We in Nuremberg cherish all that is beautiful and good. To show the world how highly we value art, I have decreed a valuable prize. Before all the people of our city, I declare that he who wins the prize in art-singing will have Eva, my own child, in marriage."

The Masters praise Veit Pogner and his worthy daughter.

"Who will enter his name as competitor?" asks Kothner.

"Not I," laughs Hans Sachs, a close friend of the Pogners. "A younger man than Beckmesser or myself must woo, if Eva is to bestow her hand."

"Speak for yourself, cobbler," snaps Beckmesser.

"If anyone seeks trial, let him step forward," calls Kothner.

Pogner introduces Walther, and the Masters agree to let him audition. Bowing before the knight, Beckmesser, the marker, smugly explains the scoring process.

"You are allowed seven faults, which I will mark on the board in chalk. If you make more than seven mistakes, you are unsung and outdone." He disappears behind the black curtain into the marker's box.

"Begin!" commands Beckmesser.

Walther sits in the singer's chair, as is the custom, and bursts enthusiastically into song. To vibrant chords, he improvises about life in spring bursting forth from the dormant forest. Walther's aria is uncommonly beautiful, but to the Masters' ears it sounds discordant and strange. Only Sachs listens with respect. The sound of Beckmesser's chalk scratching the blackboard can he heard, but Walther sings on. Unable to contain his zeal, he rises from the singer's chair, and the scandalized guild members insist he return to his seat.

Beckmesser tears open the curtain.

"Have you finished yet?" he asks spitefully, interrupting the knight's song. "There's no more room on the slate."

The Masters burst into laughter. Walther begs to complete his song.

"You're done here. You've sung your chance away," jeers the clerk, tallying the errors.

"Nothing but ear-splitting din!" concur the Masters.

"The knight's song and melody I found new but not confused," interjects Sachs. "If you need to measure by rules, perhaps you should find out what his rules are."

Sachs proposes they listen to the rest of Walther's song, but the enraged Beckmesser protests.

"Perhaps the marker's judgment is biased, since he plans to serenade Eva at the song contest," comments Sachs.

Escorting Walther back to the singer's chair, Sachs urges him to proceed in open defiance of the marker. As Walther continues his aria, Beckmesser criticizes every tone and word of the knight's song.

The Masters sing out their final decision, voting against the youth. While Sachs applauds the knight as a poet-hero, Pogner, regretting his colleagues' decision, worries for his daughter's happiness. Walther, exasperated and defiant, sings his farewell to the Masters and runs from the church.

Act II

As the sun sets that evening, David hangs a garland of flowers over Sachs's workshop door. He doesn't see Magdalene tiptoe out of the goldsmith's house across the alley. She carries a basket of cakes and sausages on her arm.

"Psst, David," she whispers, "tell me how the knight fared."

"Lene, it's a sad story. He is unsung and undone!"

"What?!" she cries, snatching the basket from his hands and running back into Pogner's house.

Sachs walks down the street and chases David into the house to work on Beckmesser's new shoes. Arm in arm, Eva and her father return from an evening's stroll. As her father climbs the stairs to his door, Magdalene appears.

"David thinks the knight has failed," she breathlessly tells Eva.

"Oh no! What am I to do? Where can we learn more?"

Magdalene suggests they speak to Hans Sachs, and Eva resolves to see him after dinner. They enter the house.

In his shop, Hans Sachs dons a leather apron as David sets the workbench next to the door. With the top half of the door open, the cobbler commands a full view of the alley, the street, and Pogner's front steps. He then sends his apprentice off to bed.

However, the cobbler has little taste for work. He reflects on the elusive beauty of Walther's song, deciding finally that its merits are sufficient to overcome the oddness of its composition. Slapping his thigh, he now sets to work. But no sooner does he hammer Beckmesser's shoe than Eva tiptoes across the cobblestones. Sachs assumes she has come for a last-minute fitting of her bridal shoes.

"And who might be the groom I'll wear them for?"

"Everyone knows Herr Beckmesser intends to win you."

"Might not a widower woo me, instead?" she asks, smiling warmly at her beloved friend.

"My child, this widower is too old for you."

"But how can you allow Beckmesser to win me at the singing contest tomorrow?"

Sachs hasn't an answer to satisfy Eva. "I'm distracted tonight," he says apologetically. "A nobleman's song-trial distressed me."

Eva asks the cobbler how Walther fared, and Sachs confirms her fears: the knight sang his chance away.

"Then why not help him compose a Mastersong?"

The cobbler wishes to test Eva's feelings before consenting to offer his help and pretends to dislike the knight. Eva runs home in tears.

With a bemused smile, Sachs nods. "Just as I thought. Now I must find a way." And he disappears into his workshop.

Meanwhile, Magdalene intercepts the distraught girl at her door to say that Herr Beckmesser plans to serenade her. The nurse tries to draw Eva inside, but she insists on waiting for Walther. He soon hastens down the alley. Downcast by the events of the

DIE MEISTERSINGER VON NÜRNBERG

day, he sings spitefully of the Mastersingers, whom he envisions as evil spirits, mocking him and stealing away his love.

"There's no hope," he tells Eva. "I beseech you, come away with me."

Agreeing to elope with him, Eva follows Magdalene inside to get ready. Walther hides behind a tree to wait, as the night watchman strolls down the street.

Hans Sachs, who has overheard their conversation, opens his door wider, shading his light to hide his presence.

"Foolish children, they musn't elope."

A figure emerges from the Pogner house—it is Eva, dressed in Magdalene's clothes. Sachs is not fooled by her disguise. Just as Walther and Eva are about to flee, the cobbler sends a beam of light into the street, illuminating the young couple.

"Hide!" pleads Eva. "Don't let him see us!"

At that moment, Sixtus Beckmesser slinks down the alley. Sachs decides to use the clerk's presence for his own purposes. Beckmesser stands beneath Eva's window and is about to sing, when the shoemaker begins hammering on his last.

"Oho! Tralalei! Tralalei! Oho!" Sachs bellows heartily.

"Why are you working so late?" demands the irritated Beckmesser.

"I'm finishing your new shoes."

Once again, Sachs sings his cobbling song, marking time with his hammer. Beckmesser covers his ears and begs Sachs to stop, but to no avail.

The window of Pogner's house opens, and Magdalene, disguised as Eva, leans out. Beckmesser again strums the lute, but the instrument can barely be heard above Sachs's hammering. The clerk begs Sachs to cease pounding. The cobbler agrees on one condition: he insists on marking the clerk's song with taps of the hammer.

No sooner has Beckmesser sung the first bar than Sachs marks him with a loud rap. Disconcerted, the clerk continues, but each line meets with a hammer blow. In a panic, the clerk sings faster, trying to get the words out before the cobbler can hammer. But the faster Beckmesser sings, the faster Sachs knocks, until he is tapping the shoe in time to the music.

The cacophony finally disturbs the neighbors, who open their windows and peep out. David looks up at Pogner's window and recognizes Magdalene.

"So, she prefers that man to me!"

Armed with a cudgel, he leaps from his window and throws himself on Beckmesser. Magdalene screams. The neighbors come from their houses to help, but instead of stopping the fight, they are drawn into the fray.

Walther and Eva come out from hiding and force a path through the mob. Sachs, who has been watching for them, grabs Walther by the arm and pushes Eva toward her doorstep. Collaring David, Sachs kicks him through the shop door and pulls Walther across the threshold. Beckmesser staggers away, and the neighbors return to their homes.

Continuing his rounds, the watchman surveys the street.

"The clock has struck eleven," he sings. "Let no evil spirit ensnare your soul." And blowing his horn, he disappears up the peaceful alley.

Act III

Hans Sachs sits at his desk, studying the pages before him. Morning sun streams through the window, lighting up his pensive face.

David tiptoes into the workshop, carrying Magdalene's basket of food. The cobbler finally notices David, and he rubs his eyes and smiles.

"Do you know your poem for the festival?" he asks.

David proudly recites his verse, and Sachs congratulates him, appointing him herald. Overjoyed, David hurries off to his room to dress for the festival.

Sachs grows thoughtful again, and, to a brooding melody, he reflects on the madness in men's souls. But when he decides to shape the madness into something nobler by helping two young people find happiness, the somber music brightens.

Refreshed after a night's sleep, Walther enters the workshop.

"I had a beautiful dream," he tells Sachs.

"That bodes well. Tell it to me and we shall fashion your dream into a Mastersong."

Walther reminds Sachs of his failure at the song trial, but the cobbler still has hope.

"Your song made the Masters uneasy and rightly so; for, when you think of it, it is with such poetry that daughters are tempted by adventure. For loving wedlock, other words and melodies were invented."

And so Sachs takes pen in hand and prepares to record the knight's dreamsong according to the Masters' rules. This song is more seasoned than the first, its beauty glowing through every word.

Shining in the rosy light of morning,
the air heavy
with blossom and scent,

full of every
unthought-of joy
a garden invited me
to be its guest.

Sachs asks Walther to compose a second stanza, and, as the knight sings on, Sachs learns as much from the youth as the youth does from the Master, until finally a Mastersong is born. Then, arm in arm, they leave to dress for the song contest.

Sixtus Beckmesser hobbles down the alley and slips through the door of Sachs's workshop. Picking up the paper he finds on the cobbler's desk, he reads the poem with great agitation.

"A wooing song by Sachs!" he exclaims. "Now I understand everything."

Hearing footsteps, he stuffs the paper in his pocket. Sachs, in a handsomely braided coat, enters the room. Beckmesser accuses the cobbler of sabotaging his efforts to win Eva, and he produces the poem as proof. The clerk's thievery gives Sachs an idea.

"So that people don't think ill of you for taking what is not yours, keep the paper. Let it be a present from me to you."

Thinking a poem by the esteemed cobbler will ensure his victory in the contest, Beckmesser throws his arms around Sachs.

"Swear you will never claim authorship of this verse," demands the clerk.

"I swear it! But I earnestly advise you to study the song carefully. It will not be easy to find the right melody and proper tone."

Sure of his success, the delighted Beckmesser rushes off.

Gazing out of the window, Sachs sees Eva approaching. She has come to complain that her shoe pinches, but Sachs understands why she is really there. The door suddenly opens and Walther enters. They stare in fascination at one another.

"I've heard a very beautiful song today," comments Sachs. "It only needs a third verse to be complete."

Walther sings, never taking his eyes off Eva:

Did the stars linger
in their lovely dance?
So light and clear
in her hair
lay with delicate gleam
a garland of stars.

"Listen, child," Sachs tells Eva, "that is a Mastersong."

The poetry and melody move Eva to tears.

"How can I reward you, dearest friend?" responds Eva tenderly. "If fate had not brought Walther to me, I would choose you for my husband."

Bedecked in ribbons and flowers, Magdalene and David enter the room. Festive music rings out as Sachs christens Walther's Mastersong "The Heavenly Morning Dream True Story."

So that he may act as witness to the christening of Walther's song, Sachs promotes David from apprentice to journeyman. Magdalene and David thank Sachs for their good fortune and vow to be married.

As the "Heavenly Morning" melody weaves in and out, everyone sings joyously, looking forward to the fulfillment of their dreams.

*   *   *

The townsfolk gather in a sunny meadow to celebrate the feast of St. John's Day. Waving their flags, members of the various guilds march past, singing a tribute to their professions.

Finally, the Mastersingers' theme echoes in the distance. With Kothner carrying their banner, the Masters march into the meadow. Veit Pogner escorts Eva to the chair of honor, and Sachs, the master of ceremonies, takes the podium.

"Today, Veit Pogner bestows a rare prize. Whoever shall succeed, let him be pure and noble of heart, so that this lovely maiden shall never regret that Nuremberg honors art and its Masters."

Stepping forward, Kothner calls for the contestants to prepare themselves.

"The eldest shall appear first. Herr Beckmesser, begin."

After a few notes on the lute, Beckmesser sings. To everyone's amazement, not only does he forget the words, but his melody is garbled and confused. The crowd laughs him off the podium.

"It's not my song!" shrieks Beckmesser, and he angrily tosses the paper at Sachs's feet. "The cobbler has palmed off his dreadful verse on me!"

Knowing Sachs incapable of composing such nonsense, everyone begs him to explain. To their astonishment, the cobbler insists that he could never have written so beautiful a song. He declares that whoever can sing the words and music properly will show that he is the author and deserves the title of Mastersinger.

Walther steps forward. His noble bearing pleases the audience, and even the Mastersingers are curious to see if the knight can make a Mastersong out of Beckmesser's gibberish. As Walther sings the first stanza of the "Heavenly Morning" song, not a murmur can be heard among the expectant throng.

With the second verse, Mastersingers and public alike marvel at the beauty of the song. As Walther sings the last verse, the crowd cries out: "Give him the wreath! He has won the prize!"

"Yes, gracious singer! Your song has won you the Masters' prize," declare the guild members unanimously. Even Beckmesser has to agree.

"No one can woo so charmingly as you, Sir Knight," sings Eva, as she places a laurel wreath on his head.

Carrying a gold chain with three medallions, Veit Pogner invites Walther to accept the necklace and join the guild of Masters. To the astonishment of Eva and the crowd, he refuses.

Sachs addresses Walther gravely, as the theme of the Mastersingers rings out.

"Not to your noble ancestors but to the Masters and your art do you owe your present happiness. How can the art that embraces such a prize be unworthy?"

Describing the importance of the guild to the survival of German art, Sachs makes a deep impression on Walther, and he humbly accepts the medallions. Then one and all hail Sachs, paying tribute to the man whose wisdom and noble feelings have prevailed on this glorious day.

The curtain falls

Tonio~"Taddeo"   Beppe~"Arlecchino"   Canio~"Pagliaccio"   Nedda~"Colombina"   Silvio

Prologue

Tonio the hunchback, dressed as the clown Taddeo, pokes his head out from behind the stage curtain. In a rich baritone, he introduces the evening's drama, telling the audience that they will see love's passion, cruelty, and despair.

"But when you look upon our tawdry costumes, don't forget real hearts beat underneath. We are stumbling through this lonely world just as you are."

Having urged the audience to watch the story unfold, Tonio vanishes behind the curtain.

Act I

On the outskirts of a small town in southern Italy, the villagers celebrate the arrival of the commedia dell'arte players, a troupe of traveling comedians. The company's tent has already been pitched and their theater assembled.

"Here they come! The clowns are back!" sings the ebullient crowd.

As the boys toss their caps high into the air, Tonio, in his clown suit, somersaults toward them. Beppe, dressed as Arlecchino, rides into the square on his donkey, drawing a brightly decorated cart. The wagon comes to a halt, its garishly painted sides contrasting vividly with the hot lemon-colored sky.

Seated in the cart is Canio, the leader of the clowns, in his Pagliaccio costume. His pretty young wife, Nedda, is the Colombina of the troupe.

"Hail the prince of clowns! Welcome, Pagliaccio!" roars the crowd.

Canio bangs loudly on his drum for silence.

"Ladies and gentlemen," he sings in a robust tenor. "Tonight you will see a spectacular show. You'll witness the sorrow and rage of Pagliaccio, taking revenge on whoever betrays him."

Cheering madly, the villagers promise to attend. Canio jumps down from the wagon and bows. He turns to help his wife from her seat, and discovers Tonio lifting Nedda out of the cart.

"Get away!" shouts Canio, pushing Tonio aside and taking Nedda in his arms, while the crowd hurls insults at the unfortunate Tonio. The humiliated clown shakes his fist and walks away, vowing to get even with Canio.

One of the spectators invites the actors to have a drink at the tavern. Canio and Beppe accept, but Tonio declines.

"Careful, Pagliaccio," teases a villager. "He's staying behind to flirt with Nedda."

Canio cautions the villager not to confuse theater with real life.

"On stage, if my wife has a boyfriend, I only give her a scolding. But if Nedda betrayed me in real life, the story would end differently."

To emphasize his point, Canio grabs the man by his lapels and wags a reproachful finger at him. Nedda watches her husband fearfully, wondering if he suspects her carefully guarded secret.

As the sun begins to set, the church bells call the townspeople to vespers, and Canio and Beppe head for the tavern with their drinking companions. Nedda remains alone, worrying that her husband has read her thoughts.

"If he knew my secret, he'd have no mercy." She stretches out on the wooden platform of their makeshift stage to bask in the sun's last rays. "I feel full of longing and life, like the birds flying overhead. They also follow a dream, an illusion."

Tonio comes out from the tent and listens in rapture to Nedda's song.

"Still here?" Nedda asks sharply, disturbed by the intrusion. "I thought you'd gone to the tavern."

Tonio pleads with Nedda to notice him.

"I know I'm ugly and deformed, that I arouse your scorn, yet I too have a dream and a desire."

But the more fervently Tonio sings, the more Nedda mocks him. He pulls her roughly to him, and, struggling free, Nedda backs toward the tent. She grabs the donkey whip and lashes out at Tonio, slicing his cheek.

"I swear you'll pay for this!" he shrieks, staggering behind the tent to nurse his wound.

A man approaches, calling Nedda's name. Violins play a soothing melody as Silvio, Nedda's secret love, embraces her tenderly. Tonio, meanwhile, has crept out from behind the tent and observes the lovers with bitter satisfaction. He hurries off to warn Canio, his scheme of revenge under way.

Silvio tries with all his might to convince Nedda to run away with him. The words of his song move her, and she at last agrees to follow him anywhere.

At that moment, Tonio leads Canio down the path toward the tent, cautioning the jealous husband to step quietly if he wants to surprise his unfaithful wife.

Silvio and Nedda make plans to go away together after the evening's performance. As Silvio leaves, Nedda calls after him.

"Until midnight, my darling, when I'll be yours forevermore."

Canio is close enough to hear Nedda's declaration—words that seal her fate. He leaps from the shadows, pushes Nedda aside, and runs after Silvio. Tonio's evil laugh tells Nedda that he is responsible for Canio's sudden appearance.

"You disgust and repel me!" she cries, spitting in his face.

"Your hatred means nothing to me," he smirks.

Canio returns without having seen the face of Nedda's mysterious lover.

"Ridiculed and disgraced," he rants. "I should slit your throat this minute, but first I must know his name!"

"I'll never tell you."

With his dagger drawn, Canio throws himself upon his wife. Beppe comes back just in time to witness the violent scene, and he quickly separates them. Tonio takes hold of Canio while Beppe leads Nedda away. Whispering in Canio's ear, Tonio counsels him to go on with the show.

"Her lover will come to the performance and then we'll unmask him. You must pretend now in order to succeed later."

Beppe now urges Canio to get dressed and tells Tonio to beat his drum until the players are ready. Both Tonio and Beppe disappear behind the theater, leaving Canio alone.

"Perform when I'm going out of my mind? Yet I must force myself. I'm a man, after all," Canio sings tearfully, walking under a flap of the tent and pulling his clown suit off a hook.

Sitting at his dressing table, he opens a jar of white greasepaint and peers into the mirror.

"Get into your costume and smear your face with paint. The people paid their money and they want to be amused. And if Arlecchino steals away your Colombina, everyone will applaud."

He rubs makeup on his cheeks, and gazes at his tired, careworn image in the mirror.

"Laugh, clown, although your love has been destroyed!"

Canio's voice rises from the depths of his tortured soul. Wringing his hands, he sobs uncontrollably. Then, dragging his costume in the dust, he staggers into the theater.

Act II

Tonio, dressed as Taddeo, beats his drum, summoning the villagers to the evening's comedy. As the excitement rises, the audience clamors, "We are all here. Let the show begin."

They quiet down when a bell rings, and the curtain rises on a little domestic scene. A wooden table and two chairs stand in front of a painted backdrop, representing a room in Colombina's house.

Nedda, in her Colombina costume, is preparing for a rendezvous with Arlecchino while her husband, Pagliaccio, is away. A guitar summons Colombina to the window, and she draws the curtains to find Arlecchino, played by Beppe, blowing her kisses.

Intending to signal her lover when it is safe, Colombina closes the curtains and sits down at the table with her back to the door. The servant Taddeo enters, unseen by his mistress. Gazing at Colombina, he sighs with longing and pathetically bats his eyelashes. The audience giggles with delight.

"Well, stupid, is Pagliaccio gone?" she asks.

"He's gone, and here is the chicken you wanted."

"Don't bother me," she snaps, hitting him on the head with the chicken before signaling to Arlecchino.

"You're so cruel, yet I can't resist you," trills Taddeo.

In a flash, Arlecchino leaps onto the stage and boxes Taddeo's ears.

"I suppose they'll hardly miss me," the servant muses. He blesses the couple and promises to keep watch outside the door, lest Pagliaccio return early.

The lovers embrace, then sit down to supper. At that moment, Taddeo bursts into the room and screams that Pagliaccio has returned in a jealous frenzy, swearing to kill his unfaithful wife.

Taddeo dives headfirst through the doorway, while Colombina helps Arlecchino climb out of the window. Canio, in his Pagliaccio costume, stands poised at the door in full view of the audience, ready to make his entrance.

"Until midnight, when I'll be yours forevermore!" Colombina sings to the departing Arlecchino.

When Canio hears these words, the very same that Nedda used earlier to her real lover, he cries out in pain. The music turns ominous as he enters the room and accuses her of entertaining a strange man.

"What nonsense! You've been drinking," replies Colombina gaily. Nedda, however, senses Canio's rage under his painted smile.

"Why are two places set at the table?" he asks, following the script.

"Taddeo sat beside me, but you scared him away."

The hunchback sticks his head through the door and feigns terror while speaking his lines with pointed sarcasm.

"How could such a faithful wife tell a lie?"

PAGLIACCI · ACT I

The audience laughs, but for the last time. No sooner does Tonio disappear than Canio, goaded by the hunchback's remark, grabs Nedda's wrists.

"By heaven, Nedda, I want his name!"

Trying to remain in character, Nedda smiles nervously and replies, "But whose?"

"The vile man who held you in his arms," he answers vengefully, tearing off his clown hat and throwing it to the floor. "If my face is chalk white, it's from the shame of my dishonor. This disgrace can only be washed away by blood."

He circles round Nedda, driven by his anger.

"When you were dying of hunger, I gave you a home, a name, and love," he laments.

Canio's grief is so real that the audience is moved to tears, marveling at the brilliance of his performance. But Silvio, watching from the back of the audience, grows uneasy.

"I believed in you," Canio sings in a voice choked with sorrow. "Now you'll feel my revenge!"

"If you think me so unworthy, why don't you send me away?"

"Never! You'll stay here and tell me his name."

Silvio wrings his hands, unsure of what to do. Nedda resumes the play, and, in a quavering soprano, she tries to make light of her terror.

"He was only the harmless Arlecchino," she sings softly.

Her acting momentarily reassures Silvio, and he steps back into the shadows. But Canio, enraged by her behavior, howls, "Don't you understand? Tell me his name or I'll kill you!"

Nedda courageously replies, "Though you despise me, my love is stronger than your hatred. I will not speak, even if you kill me."

Picking up a knife from the table, Canio points it at his wife. The spectators finally realize what is happening and rise from their seats in horror, obstructing Silvio's desperate attempt to reach the stage.

Nedda runs into the crowd, pursued by Canio. Before she can escape, her husband overtakes her and stabs her in the back.

"Help me, Silvio!" Nedda cries out—her last words.

When Silvio finally reaches Nedda and calls her name, Canio stabs him savagely in the chest. Then, his face a mask of horror, Canio opens his hand, letting the knife drop to the ground.

"The comedy is ended!" chants Tonio as Pagliaccio's theme is heard again and the grieving clown clasps Nedda in his arms.

The curtain falls

GEORGE GERSHWIN

PORGY AND BESS

Sporting Life

Serena

Porgy

Crown

Bess

Act I

On a hot summer night in the 1920s, couples dance in the courtyard of Catfish Row, a black neighborhood on the waterfront of Charleston, South Carolina.

Clara, the wife of Jake the fisherman, rocks her baby and sings "Summertime," a poignant lullaby. Nearby, a crap game is under way, the participants chanting, "Roll dem bones, roll," as they wait for the throw of the dice. Serena, Robbins's wife, begs her husband not to join the game, but he picks up the dice anyway.

Convinced he can better soothe their child, Jake takes his son from Clara and, to a jazzy melody, lectures him about women and the perils of marriage. Jake's friends join the chorus, much to Clara's annoyance. When the baby wails, the men laugh and Clara carries him away.

Old Peter, the honey man, enters the courtyard, balancing a tray of honeycomb on his head. He is followed by Porgy, a crippled beggar, who rides his goat cart through the gates and is greeted warmly by his friends.

"Lay down your money, Porgy," calls Sporting Life, a drug peddler from New York.

"Roll 'em," demands Robbins impatiently.

But Mingo, another player, cautions them to wait for Crown who is on his way and in a foul mood. Porgy asks if Crown's girlfriend, Bess, will be with him, and the men all laugh, suspecting that Porgy is sweet on Bess. Porgy protests, claiming a cripple is meant to be lonely.

"Night time, day time, he got to trabble dat lonesome road," he sings sadly.

The frightened yells of the neighborhood children reach their ears as the brutish Crown enters the courtyard with Bess on his arm. She is dressed in red silk, in sharp contrast to the subdued calicos of the other women.

Crown impatiently throws down his money, and the game begins in earnest. Drinking steadily, Crown challenges every roll of the dice.

Robbins, on a winning streak, shakes the dice, praying for a nine. When he rolls his number, he excitedly sweeps up his winnings from the pile of money on the ground.

Seizing Robbins by the wrist, Crown, in a drunken rage, threatens to kill him. Robbins runs up a flight of stairs, but he can't escape. Crown kicks him down the stairs and they scuffle at the bottom. When Robbins picks up a brick and lunges at Crown, the drunkard pulls out his cotton hook and stabs his rival to death.

Serena screams and falls on her husband's body. The witnesses flee in all directions.

"You done kill Robbins and the police will be comin'," Bess cries, shaking Crown to his senses.

"Where you goin' hide?" he asks Bess.

"Some man always willin' to take care of Bess."

"Whoever he is, he's temporary. I's comin' back."

No sooner does Crown disappear than Sporting Life approaches Bess.

"Listen, I'll be goin' to New York soon. I'll hide you out and take you with me."

Bess refuses to go, but she does accept some happy dust from Sporting Life's outstretched hand.

When the police whistle blows, the dope peddler dashes off, leaving Bess alone and frightened. She runs from door to door begging for shelter, but no one will let her in. Suddenly, a light gleams in Porgy's window, the door opens, and the beggar, on his knees, extends his hand. Bess staggers toward his door, and Porgy, reaching for her hand, pulls her inside.

*   *   *

A bell tolls as mourners file into Serena's room to pay their last respects to Robbins. The dead man lies on a bed, a saucer filled with coins balanced on his chest.

To Serena's surprise, Bess accompanies Porgy into the room and drops money into the saucer. Leading his friends in a rhythmic spiritual, Porgy urges them to fill the saucer till it overflows, so that Serena can pay for her husband's funeral.

They are interrupted by the Detective, who is investigating Robbins's murder. Trying to get the group to name the real killer, he turns on old Peter and accuses him of the crime.

Fearing imprisonment, Peter names Crown. Because Porgy's hut opens onto the court, the Detective questions the cripple as well. Porgy, however, refuses to answer, swearing he was asleep when the murder was committed. Seizing Peter as a material witness, the Detective leaves, planning to hold the old man until Crown is found.

Bess leads the mourners in a rousing spiritual, and their hopes rise anew despite the tragedy in their midst. No longer treating Bess as an outsider, the people of Catfish Row now welcome her as a friend and neighbor.

Act II

On a September morning, Jake and the other fishermen repair their nets in the courtyard of Catfish Row. Though the stormy season is at hand, they resolve to cast off for the Blackfish banks as soon as possible.

"It take a long pull to get there," they sing heartily. "But I'll anchor in the Promise' Lan'."

Porgy leans out of his window to see what is going on and, to the sound of a banjo, sings joyously: "Oh, I got plenty of nuttin', an' nuttin's plenty fo' me."

Busy at their morning chores, the neighborhood women listen to Porgy's song and agree that he is happy now that Bess has come to stay.

Sporting Life, strutting about the court in his fancy suit and spats, saunters toward the cookshop and eyes Maria, the owner. Noticing the white powder in the palm of his hand, Maria angrily blows the dust into the air. She grabs the dope peddler and puts a carving knife to his throat, warning him not to peddle happy dust around her shop again. Sporting Life squirms out of Maria's grip and runs off.

Moments later, a white visitor appears on Catfish Row asking for Porgy. Mr. Archdale, a friend of Peter's, offers to post the old man's bail and return him to his family. After thanking Archdale, Porgy goes inside. His neighbors return home to change for the church picnic and Bess is left alone in the court.

Sporting Life strolls back into the square and again offers to take Bess to New York. Again she refuses. When he tries to tempt her with happy dust, she resists. Porgy, from inside his room, overhears their conversation and quietly opens the door. He reaches around, grabbing Sporting Life by the wrist in a vise-like grip.

"You keep away from my woman, or I'll break yo' neck!" shouts Porgy, scaring the dope peddler away.

Porgy has now proven to himself and to Bess that he can protect her.

"Bess, you is my woman now!" he sings, taking her in his arms. "An' you mus' laugh an' sing an' dance for two instead of one."

Bess responds, singing of her devotion to Porgy, and, in a touching duet, they pledge to love each other forever.

Dressed in their Sunday best for the picnic on Kittiwah Island, the inhabitants of Catfish Row converge on the courtyard and head for the boat, but Bess lingers behind to keep the crippled Porgy company.

Maria insists Bess come along, and Porgy, too, tells Bess to go. Bidding him a tender farewell, Bess leaves with Maria as Porgy, waving happily, sings, "Got my gal, got my Lawd, got my song!"

*   *   *

On Kittiwah Island, everyone dances to the rhythmic beat of African drums. Sporting Life then leads the picnickers in song, and, responding to the insinuating tune and outrageous words, they all join in the chorus. Serena scolds them for their wicked behavior.

As the stars appear in the sky, the steamboat whistle blows, calling the passengers to embark for home. Bess is the last to leave the clearing. Crown, who has been hiding on the island, jumps out from a thicket. Bess, shocked to see her old lover, backs away. She tells him that she now lives with Porgy and intends to go back to Catfish Row.

"In a couple ob weeks I's comin' for you, you gets dat?" says Crown, grabbing her roughly.

Unable to resist, Bess ignores the final boat whistle and stays behind with Crown.

*   *   *

Just before daybreak on Catfish Row, Jake and the fishermen prepare to set out to sea. Clara kisses her husband and watches apprehensively as they disappear from sight.

Delirious with fever, Bess cries out from Porgy's room. After two days on Kittiwah Island, she returned home and has been semiconscious for over a week.

Maria and Serena wait with Porgy outside his door. Old Peter, out on bail, returns to the square and joins Porgy and the women in a prayer for Bess. As a bell chimes five o'clock, Bess's fever breaks and she calls out to Porgy.

"Thank Gawd!" cries Porgy as Bess appears in the doorway.

Porgy knows she has seen Crown on the island, but he promises to care for her no matter what has happened.

"I loves you, Porgy," she sings tenderly, begging him to protect her from Crown.

"When Crown come, that's my business! You got a home now, honey, an' you got love."

Resting her weary head on Porgy's shoulder, Bess goes with him into the room.

Clara, returning from the wharf, tells Maria she has never seen the water look so black. Suddenly the wind rises, the sky darkens, and the hurricane bell tolls. The inhabitants cry out in terror and race to their doors.

"Jake, Jake!" cries Clara, fainting in Maria's arms.

*   *   *

In Serena's room, everyone huddles together to wait out the storm and pray for their loved ones. Clara holds her baby close, singing "Summertime" to soothe the child.

As thunder rolls, the fearful crowd sings, "Oh, dere's somebody knockin' at de do'."

Peter answers that he hears death knocking. Suddenly, several real knocks are heard and the door rattles violently. The men push against it with all their might, but finally

the door gives way, driving them to the floor. The wind shrieks, water splashes into the room, and Crown appears before them.

He eyes the crowd and discovers Bess sitting beside Porgy. "Ain' dere no whole men left?" he asks, grabbing Bess.

Porgy attempts to protect her, but Crown throws him to the floor. An indignant Serena warns Crown to behave himself or God will strike him dead.

As the group reprimands him for disturbing their prayers, Clara, who has been staring out of the window, screams. Bess rushes to her side and sees Jake's fishing boat overturned in the water. Clara hands the baby to Bess and runs out into the storm.

"Won't somebody go to Clara? Ain't dere no man here?" cries Bess in desperation.

Crown, the only one brave enough to step forward, disappears into the raging storm after Clara.

*   *   *

It is dusk on Catfish Row and the inhabitants mourn those lost in the storm, praying for the souls of Clara, Jake, and Crown. Sporting Life staggers drunkenly toward them, laughing heartily at their prayers for Crown.

The music darkens as Crown sneaks into the court and creeps toward Porgy's door. As he passes under the window, a hand grasping a dagger reaches out and stabs Crown in the back. Crown staggers to his feet, and Porgy leans out of the window, seizing him by the neck. They struggle, and Porgy strangles him.

Calling Bess, Porgy laughs triumphantly, "You got a man now, you got Porgy!"

*   *   *

The next afternoon, the Detective returns to Catfish Row, accompanied by the coroner. Climbing the stairs to Serena's room, he knocks on her door, intending to question Robbins's widow about Crown's murder. He is greeted by her friends, Annie and Lily, who swear the widow has been sick in bed for three days and knows nothing. When Serena finally appears, she confirms their story and the coroner declares their alibi airtight. He still needs someone to identify the body, however, and he picks Porgy.

Because Porgy is superstitious, he is afraid to look at a dead man's face. Bess tries to reassure him, but Sporting Life, who has been eavesdropping, terrifies Porgy.

"When the man that killed Crown go in that room—an' look at him, Crown' wound begin to bleed!"

Two policemen enter the square and drag Porgy off to the morgue. Sporting Life then frightens Bess by insisting that Porgy will be charged with Crown's murder and locked up in jail for years.

Bess trembles. The scoundrel takes advantage of her helplessness and offers her happy dust. At first she refuses, but then she gives in and takes it. With Bess now in his power, Sporting Life sings a jaunty song about life in New York.

"There's a boat dat's leavin' soon for New York. Come wid me, dat's where we belong, sister."

Bess comes to her senses and refuses a second offer of happy dust. She curses Sporting Life and runs into the hut, slamming the door behind her. Sporting Life leaves a packet of the white powder on her doorstep, certain she will come out later to get it.

*   *   *

A week has passed since Porgy left. Life on Catfish Row is back to normal, and the neighbors sing out their good mornings.

The clang of a patrol wagon is heard and Mingo, looking past the iron gate, sees Porgy. His friends gaze apprehensively at the gate, but they greet Porgy warmly when he appears.

"Ain' I tell you, I ain' goin' look on Crown's face. I keep dese eyes shut in dat room 'til they done put me in jail for contemp' of court."

Porgy's week in jail served him well. Lucky at gambling, he won enough money to buy presents for all his friends. When he holds up a red dress for Bess, his neighbors grow uncomfortable and begin to disperse. Porgy realizes something is wrong. He runs into his room, calling frantically for Bess, and discovers she is gone.

"Where's my Bess?" he asks tragically.

"She gone. She gave herself to de debbil," Serena answers. "Try forget 'bout Bess."

When Porgy learns that Bess has gone to New York, he resolves to follow her and calls for his goat and cart. Knowing the chance of finding Bess is slight, his friends beg him to stay on Catfish Row, but he ignores their advice.

"Oh Lawd, I'm on my way. I'm on my way to a Heav'nly Lan'," Porgy sings, and his friends join the rousing spiritual as he drives away from Catfish Row.

The curtain falls

Prologue

Next to the Nuremberg opera house stands Luther's Tavern, a favorite haunt of students, poets, and artists. On the evening of the prima donna Stella's debut in *Don Giovanni*, Councilor Lindorf, a tall, imposing man, enters the tavern. He is just in time to intercept a letter from Stella to the poet Hoffmann.

To the poignant sound of violins, Lindorf reads: "I love you. If you love me and I have made you suffer—forgive me."

Inside the envelope, Lindorf finds the key to Stella's dressing room. Pocketing it, the councilor chuckles diabolically and wonders why women give their love to drunken fools and poor poets. Addressing himself to a portrait of Stella which hangs on the tavern wall, he swears to subdue his rival, Hoffmann, and win Stella for his own. He glances at his watch, notes the time, and retreats into the shadows to observe from afar the entrance of the poet.

Applause from the opera house signals the intermission. Luther readies his waiters as a stream of excited students pours down the tavern steps calling for wine and beer.

"Fill our glasses until dawn," they demand, taking seats around the long, wooden tables. Full of good humor, they sing an ode to the innkeeper and his cellar, their robust voices rising in the spirit of fraternity. One of the students, Nathanael, gazes at the portrait of Stella and proposes a toast to the singer—a toast promptly echoed by his friends.

"But why isn't Hoffmann here?" asks Hermann, another student.

At that moment, Hoffmann and his devoted companion, Nicklausse, appear at the top of the stairs. The poet is unshaven, bedraggled, and already drunk. He stumbles down the tavern steps and sits at a table, burying his head in his hands. From his seat in the shadows, Lindorf watches. Hoffmann is clearly suffering because of Stella, but the councilor has no intention of delivering her letter.

In an effort to cheer him up, Nathanael suggests that Hoffmann serenade them with a merry song. The poet begins a ballad, but his thoughts soon turn to Stella, and he is again overcome with emotion. Because he never names the object of his love, his friends sit in confused but respectful silence until he finally regains his composure. Embarrassed, he resumes the ballad, and the students join in the final refrain.

The poet calls for flaming punch—a cry that is seconded by his friends. As they fill their goblets, Nathanael remarks that surely Hoffmann must be in love.

"In love? May the devil take me if I am!"

"A rash remark. You never can tell," comments Lindorf.

Hoffmann recognizes his nemesis at once and hails him as an agent of Lucifer. Calling him a fugitive from hell, Lindorf provokes the poet, and the two men nearly come to blows. Fortunately, Nicklausse intervenes.

"Each time I meet Lindorf, something terrible happens," Hoffmann tells his friends. "If I gamble, I lose. If I drink, I choke. If I love. . . ."

Lindorf's demonic laugh resounds. "So you admit you fall in love."

Nathanael comes to Hoffmann's defense, assuring the poet that each one of them pines for someone's love. But Hoffmann denies loving a single woman.

"I love three women in one, a trio of enchantresses who share my days. Would you like to hear about them?"

When the theater bell rings, signaling the second act of *Don Giovanni*, only a few rise to leave. The rest eagerly await the unfolding of Hoffmann's tales.

"The first one's name was Olympia," the poet begins.

Act I

Olympia, a life-size mechanical doll created by Dr. Spalanzani, sits on a velvet chair in his workshop. The brilliant inventor has invited the cream of Parisian society to meet his "daughter" this evening.

"With her, I'll recover the five hundred ducats I lost when Elias went bankrupt," he confides to his servant, Cochenille. "My only worry is that my associate, Coppélius, may try and cheat me out of the money."

Hoffmann, Spalanzani's pupil, is the first to arrive for the festivities. As he enters the workshop, the inventor draws the curtains around Olympia's chair.

"Tonight, you will meet my daughter," says Spalanzani. "Science is everything, my dear fellow."

Hoffmann, who believes Olympia is real, wonders what science has to do with her. Dr. Spalanzani excuses himself, and the young man, who has already fallen in love with Olympia after seeing her through a window, decides to take a look behind the curtains. To the innocent lover, Olympia appears to be sleeping.

"How beautiful she is!" he sighs. Singing a tender song, he pleads passionately with the doll to open her heart to love.

When Hoffmann's friend Nicklausse enters the workshop, the poet drops the curtain around Olympia. Nicklausse realizes that Olympia is only made of porcelain, and he teases Hoffmann about a doll with enamel eyes who sighs, "I love you." But Nicklausse's meaning eludes Hoffmann, and he dismisses his friend's remarks.

A strange old man sneaks into the room and watches with interest as Hoffmann peers into the curtained alcove.

"I am Dr. Coppélius—a friend of Spalanzani's," he introduces himself. "Look at my barometers, hygrometers, and thermometers—all available at a discount."

Unbuttoning his overcoat, he displays the wares that are neatly sewn into its lining. His collection of eyes, however, is his most prized possession.

"I create real, living eyes. Eyes of flame that see into the depths of the soul."

From his pocket he takes a handful of eyes that look as true as life but feel as cold as marble. Coppélius then offers to sell the student a pair of rose-tinted glasses that will reveal whether his love is pure of heart. The magic spectacles alter Hoffmann's vision, and Olympia seems more lifelike than ever.

Dr. Spalanzani returns to check on his creation, and is dismayed to discover Coppélius.

"Soon it will be raining money and I want my share," snarls the old scientist.

"But I'm Olympia's father!" retorts Spalanzani.

"She has my eyes."

Spalanzani is desperate to rid himself of Coppélius, and tries a different tactic.

"Give me the rights to her eyes and to all the rest of her, and you can collect five hundred ducats from my banker, Elias."

Coppélius agrees, suggesting, with a fiendish cackle, that Spalanzani marry Olympia to the young fool who has fallen in love with her.

As Spalanzani pulls the curtains around his creation, Coppélius withdraws and Cochenille announces the arrival of the guests. To a minuet, the company enters, toasting their gracious host and begging to see his daughter.

The curtain rises, Olympia is introduced, and the crowd gasps with delight. The proud inventor circles the room with the doll, who curtsies and twirls daintily on her toes. Everyone sings her praises.

"Olympia will now perform for you," announces Spalanzani.

Olympia sings a charming aria of great delicacy, her voice hitting each note with precision: "The birds in the bower, the stars in the sky—everything speaks of love to a young girl."

When she suddenly falters, Spalanzani has no choice but to rewind her. Though the sound of a turning spring can be heard, no one seems to notice; and the audience joins the refrain, gaily singing until Olympia is able to proceed. At the conclusion, she curtsies primly as the audience applauds.

Spalanzani escorts her to her chair just as supper is announced. Excusing Olympia after her tiring performance, he asks the lovestruck Hoffmann to stay behind and keep her company. The inventor slyly winds Olympia's springs, and then beckons the guests to join him in the dining room.

The doll, mechanically waving a fan back and forth, stares into the distance as the room empties.

"They have gone away at last! Let me intoxicate myself with your bewitching look," sighs Hoffmann.

"Yes! Yes!" she responds.

Assuming that her assent is a declaration of love, the young student sings passionately, seeing Olympia through the rose-colored glasses as if in a dream. In his fervor he presses her hand, setting off a mechanism in her legs. She rises swiftly from her chair and runs frantically around the room. The mystified Hoffmann is about to follow her out of the door when Nicklausse enters.

"Control yourself!" he cries. "Come, have a drink with us."

"She loves me!"

"Upon my faith! Even the guests know she's an automaton."

But Hoffmann, carried away by love, ignores his friend and runs after her. Shaking his head, Nicklausse follows.

Coppélius pokes his head through the door and enters the empty workshop.

"Thief! Brigand!" he rages. "Elias is bankrupt. I shall find the right moment to avenge myself."

Coppélius hides in Olympia's alcove as the company returns. To the enthusiastic approval of the guests, Olympia and Hoffmann waltz, but Olympia loses the tempo, turning faster and faster and dragging Hoffmann with her. At last, the inventor manages to turn her off, and Cochenille returns her to the alcove.

As ominous chords play, the sound of breaking machinery can be heard. Dr. Coppélius emerges from the alcove carrying the broken body of Olympia. He passes the relic to Hoffmann, who cradles her in his arms, realizing at last that he had fallen in love with a mechanical doll.

Act II

In a lavish palace on Venice's Grand Canal, Nicklausse and the beautiful Giulietta join in a romantic barcarole.

"Beautiful night of love, smile upon our raptures," sings Nicklausse, and Giulietta adds her voice to the languid melody.

Beside her, on a velvet chaise, sits her companion, the hunchback, Pitichinaccio. Gondolas drift by as Giulietta's guests, some in masks and costumes, drink wine and embrace.

Hoffmann listens to the duet, but tender love holds no charm for him, and he bursts into a song of passionate romance. The guests applaud his sentiments, joining the lively refrain.

Schlémil, Giulietta's lover, suddenly returns after a three-day absence. Giulietta introduces Hoffmann, and the two men take an immediate dislike to one another. Tactfully suggesting a game of faro, Giulietta leads the party into the next room. Nicklausse detains Hoffmann for a moment.

"I have two horses waiting. When you start to dream of love, that's when I take you away."

"What dreams could be born here?" asks Hoffmann, surveying the gaudy surroundings.

Nicklausse warns his friend to be careful, reminding him that the devil is cunning. While they speak, a dark shadow looms in an upper gallery. A frightening apparition, hidden in a black cloak, descends the staircase as the two young friends adjourn to the gaming room.

Reaching the bottom of the staircase and dropping his cape, the sinister Dappertutto is revealed. The villain smiles fiendishly, vowing to possess Hoffmann's soul. From his pocket Dappertutto draws an enormous diamond ring that sparkles with an unearthly glow.

"Sparkle, diamond, like the mirror that catches the lark," he sings. "The lark loses its life, the woman loses her soul."

Like a magnet, the diamond pulls Giulietta from the gaming room to Dappertutto's side. Hypnotized, she stretches her hands toward the gem.

"What do you ask of your servant?"

"Seducer of hearts, you have given me Schlémil's shadow. Today, I want Hoffmann's reflection."

"I'll make him my plaything," she vows.

Satisfied, Dappertutto kisses Giulietta's hand and leaves. Hoffmann enters and picks up his coat.

"I've lost everything at the gaming tables," he says, bidding her goodbye.

Determined to make him stay, Giulietta feigns grief. The poet, charmed by her beauty, declares his love. Giulietta turns from him as if overcome with remorse.

"If Schlémil finds you here, he'll kill you. Leave me, and tomorrow I promise to follow you anywhere."

Hoffmann embraces her and sings of his love: "Your voice fills me with music. Your eyes burn into mine like stars."

"Before you go, give me something to remember you by."

Leading the bewildered Hoffmann to a mirror, Giulietta persuades him to look into the glass.

"Give me this reflection," she sings seductively. "It can detach itself from the glass and hide, completely whole, within my heart."

Hoffmann is powerless to refuse her and promises his reflection, his soul, his very life if she so wishes. As they kiss, Schlémil returns to the room, followed by Pitichinaccio, Dappertutto, and Nicklausse.

"She has abandoned us for Hoffmann," observes Schlémil, laughing contemptuously.

"Let's kill him," suggests Pitichinaccio.

Dappertutto approaches Hoffmann and, holding a mirror to his face, sarcastically comments, "How pale you look."

"I've lost my reflection!" cries the horrified poet.

"Let's go before you lose your soul," Nicklausse pleads.

"Never! I love her!"

Giulietta greedily takes the diamond from Dappertutto and places it on her finger. In resignation, Hoffmann curses his love for her. Joining his song, Giulietta claims to adore the poet—not enough, however, to resist a diamond that costs only a kiss.

As the music subsides, Giulietta, with Pitichinaccio in tow, steps through the door to her room. Hoffmann turns to Schlémil and demands the key to that door.

"You'll have to kill me for it," declares Schlémil, drawing his sword.

Dappertutto tosses the poet his blade and a vicious duel ensues. Though the older man fights bravely, Hoffmann prevails, and he stabs Schlémil in the chest. Taking the key from his rival's pocket, Hoffmann hurries into Giulietta's room, but she is nowhere to be found. Returning to the gallery, he discovers Giulietta and Pitichinaccio embarking in a gondola.

"What will you do with him now?" calls Dappertutto, pointing to the stupefied poet.

"I'll leave him to you," laughs Giulietta, floating out of sight to strains of the barcarole.

The faithful Nicklausse, rousing Hoffmann from his stupor, drags his friend out of the palace to safety.

Act III

Crespel, the father of Hoffmann's fiancée, Antonia, has taken her to Munich in order to separate the young couple. He fears their love poses a threat to Antonia's health.

In the gloomy drawing room of their Munich home, beneath a portrait of her mother, Antonia sits at the harpsichord and sings of her love for Hoffmann.

"The turtledove has flown away but she is still faithful. Beloved, my voice calls you. My heart is yours."

Crespel enters the room to find Antonia, who is trembling from the exertion of singing.

"Precious daughter, you promised you wouldn't sing."

"My mother came alive in me. By singing, my heart thought it was listening to her."

Crespel, tormented by the fear that Antonia will die of tuberculosis, just as her mother before her, begs his daughter to sing no more. Though singing is her dearest pleasure, Antonia promises to obey and leaves the drawing room. Crespel rues the day she fell in love with Hoffmann, blaming the poet for arousing this desire to sing.

Frantz, the deaf old servant, enters.

"Don't open the door to anybody!" shouts Crespel, leaving the house for an appointment.

Moments later, Hoffmann arrives, sneaking in through a back door. Old Frantz is delighted to see the poet and fetches Antonia.

"I knew you still loved me!" she cries.

"My heart told me you missed me."

Swearing to be married the next day, they sing of their love and their dreams for the future. Hoffmann's only worry is that Antonia loves music more than him.

"You aren't going to forbid me to sing as my father has done?"

"What do you mean?"

But Antonia ignores his question, insisting that they perform their favorite song.

"The rosebud smiles at spring, but how long will it love?" she sings in a melancholy voice, and Hoffmann joins her in a poignant duet. Faint from exhaustion, she swoons in Hoffmann's arms, but the sound of the door revives her.

"Heavens! It's my father! Follow me," she begs.

Hoffmann, however, chooses to hide in the drawing room.

No sooner does Crespel enter than the doorbell rings. Disobeying his master's instructions, Frantz opens the door and reveals Dr. Miracle standing on the threshold.

"Don't let him in," shouts Crespel. "He's more like a gravedigger than a doctor. He would kill my daughter as he did my wife."

But Crespel's pleas are to no avail. Terrified, Frantz runs off as the sinister Dr. Miracle enters the house.

"Where is Antonia?" the doctor inquires with exaggerated concern. "Is her illness progressing? We shall cure her. Bring her to me."

"So that you can make her sing and kill her? Never!"

Overhearing their conversation, Hoffmann recognizes at once the stranger's evil intention.

Dr. Miracle stretches his hand toward Antonia's room and, in deep, somber tones, asks her to come to him. With a magical wave of his hands, he commands her door to open and places the helpless girl under a trance.

"Sing!" he orders.

"No! Don't make her sing!" pleads her father.

Antonia's voice rings out from the next room. Victorious, Dr. Miracle motions for the door to close and, drawing some medicine bottles from his bag, prescribes them for Antonia's condition.

"God preserve me from your advice!" cries Crespel, finally managing to push the doctor out through the door.

But the fiend soon reappears, passing through the wall as if it were air. In a frantic trio, Miracle insists that his medicine will cure Antonia, while Crespel bids Satan leave his house and Hoffmann, still in hiding, swears to save Antonia. Finally Dr. Miracle leaves, followed by Crespel, who wants to make sure he doesn't return to destroy Antonia.

Hoffmann now realizes he must convince Antonia to give up singing. She enters the drawing room, ignorant of Miracle's visit.

"What did my father say?"

"We'll talk of that later. Now we must begin a new life together," Hoffmann tells her, and he makes her promise to give up her dreams of a singing career.

Vowing to return the next day, the poet leaves and Antonia sits down at the harpsichord.

"He has become my father's accomplice," she utters sadly, but she resolves to sing no more.

Magically reappearing, Miracle whispers in her ear: "Sing no more? Do you know what a sacrifice they are imposing on you? Must your beauty and talent be hidden away?"

"Is this the warning voice of God or the devil? No, accursed voice, my love is armed against my pride."

Pressing her hands to her ears, Antonia cries out for help to her mother's portrait. Dr. Miracle scoffs at the terrified girl, claiming that it is her mother who speaks through him. He makes the portrait come alive, and Antonia's mother materializes before her.

"She bequeaths to you a talent the world has lost. Sing!" he urges.

As Antonia sings, Dr. Miracle produces a violin and accompanies her. With terrible ferocity he plays faster and faster, compelling the girl into a frenzied song. As she clutches her heart, her mother and Miracle sing with her, urging her on till she collapses.

His hellish work finished, Miracle disappears and Antonia's mother returns to the portrait. Crespel comes home to discover his daughter lying on the floor.

"My child!" he cries in anguish.

"My mother calls me," Antonia sighs. Thinking of Hoffmann, she smiles peacefully and adds, "'Tis a love song that flies away."

These are her last words. She dies in her father's arms.

Hoffmann, entering the house with Nicklausse, is confronted by Crespel, who blames the poet for Antonia's death. Hoffmann ignores Crespel's threats and calls frantically for a doctor.

"Present!" answers a familiar voice, and Dr. Miracle reappears.

Aghast, Crespel cries out. Hoffmann holds Antonia in his arms and stares in horror at her murderer.

Epilogue

The exhausted Hoffmann concludes his tales: "The memory of these love affairs remains in my heart forever!"

Applause from the opera house brings Hoffmann's audience back to reality. Lindorf, from his table in the corner of the tavern, observes the poet.

"Hoffmann is no longer a threat," he mutters. "The diva is mine."

Heartbroken, the poet calls out, "Stella," and his friends realize that they have been listening to three dramas in one.

"They're all the same woman—maiden, courtesan, and artist," says Nicklausse. "Stella is all three."

As the students cry "La Stella," Hoffmann calls for wine, and everyone sings the rollicking drinking song once more before leaving the tavern.

Hoffmann sits slumped at a table, overcome by drink. In his misery a vision appears before him—the Muse of Poetry.

"May the storm of passions be stilled in you! The man is no more, the poet is born."

Momentarily inspired, Hoffmann lifts his head, but the vision disappears. Stella descends the staircase and calls his name, but it is too late—Hoffmann, nearly unconscious, cannot hear her.

Councilor Lindorf, approaching the diva, bows and takes her hand. Stella looks back with regret at the drunken poet, and then leaves the tavern on Lindorf's arm.

The curtain falls

Some Information on the Operas

Prepared by Donald King

Aida

Music by Giuseppe Verdi. Libretto in Italian by Antonio Ghislanzoni, based on the French prose of Camille du Locle, in turn based on a prose sketch by Auguste Mariette. First performance in Cairo on December 24, 1871.

Amahl and the Night Visitors

Music and libretto in English by Gian Carlo Menotti, based on the Hieronymus Bosch painting, The Adoration of the Magi. Commissioned and premiered by the NBC-TV Opera Theater. First performance on December 24, 1951.

The Barber of Seville

Music by Gioacchino Rossini. Libretto in Italian by Cesare Sterbini, based on the play by Beaumarchais. First performance in Rome on February 20, 1816.

La Bohème

Music by Giacomo Puccini. Libretto in Italian by Giuseppe Giacosa and Luigi Illica, based on the novel Scènes de la Vie de Bohème by Henri Murger. First performance in Turin on February 1, 1896.

Carmen

Music by Georges Bizet. Libretto in French by Henri Meilhac and Ludovic Halévy, based on the novel by Prosper Mérimée. First performance in Paris on March 3, 1875.

The Daughter of the Regiment

Music by Gaetano Donizetti. Libretto in French by Jules-Henri Vernoy de Saint-Georges and Jean-François-Alfred Bayard. First performance in Paris on February 11, 1840.

L'Enfant et les Sortilèges

Music by Maurice Ravel. Libretto in French by Colette. First performance in Monte Carlo on March 21, 1925.

Die Fledermaus

Music by Johann Strauss the Younger. Libretto in German by Carl Haffner and Richard Genée, based on a French play Le Réveillon by Henri Meilhac and Ludovic Halévy. First performance in Vienna on April 5, 1874.

Hansel and Gretel

Music by Engelbert Humperdinck. Libretto in German by Adelheid Wette (the composer's sister), based on the fairy tale by Ludwig Grimm. First performance in Weimar on December 23, 1893.

The Love for Three Oranges

Music by Sergei Prokofiev. Libretto in Russian by the composer, based on a comedy by Carlo Gozzi. First performance in Chicago on December 30, 1921.

The Magic Flute

Music by Wolfgang Amadeus Mozart. Libretto in German by Emanuel Schikaneder. First performance in Vienna on September 30, 1791.

Die Meistersinger von Nürnberg

Music and libretto in German by Richard Wagner. First performance in Munich on June 21, 1868.

Pagliacci

Music and libretto in Italian by Ruggero Leoncavallo. First performance in Milan on May 21, 1892.

Porgy and Bess

Music by George Gershwin. Libretto in English by DuBose Heyward. Lyrics by DuBose Heyward and Ira Gershwin. Based on the play Porgy by Dorothy and DuBose Heyward. First performance in Boston on September 30, 1935.

The Tales of Hoffmann

Music by Jacques Offenbach. Libretto in French by Jules Barbier from a play by Jules Barbier and Michel Carré, based on stories by E.T.A. Hoffmann. First performance (without scene in Venice) in Paris on February 10, 1881.